Her Strength, Her Story: A Woman's Guide to Navigating Divorce

Rediscovering Yourself, Rebuilding Your Life, and Embracing New Beginnings

Lijwana Washington

Chic Custom Concepts Press

Copyright © 2024 Lijwana Washington

All rights reserved

No part of this book may be reproduced, or stored in a retrieval system, or transmitted in any form or by any means, electronic, mechanical, photocopying, recording, or otherwise, without express written permission of the publisher.

ISBN: 9781666412130

Cover design by: Lijwana Washington
Printed in the United States of America

Writing this book has been a journey of reflection, resilience, and growth—much like the path of divorce itself. I am deeply grateful for the support and love of those who stood by me through every step.

To my dad, whose love and wisdom continue to guide me even in his absence. Though he is no longer here, his spirit and strength remain with me, inspiring every step of this journey. I am grateful for the values he instilled in me and the countless ways he shaped who I am today. This book is, in part, a tribute to his memory and to the unconditional support he gave me throughout his life.

To my mom, my unwavering support, and my greatest inspiration. Through every step of this journey, you have been my rock, my motivator, and my confidante. In the most challenging moments, your strength and patience gave me the courage to keep moving forward. Thank you for being there to listen, to lift me, and to remind me of my resilience. I am endlessly grateful for your love and guidance.

To my children, you are my greatest source of joy and motivation. Every day, you inspire me to keep pushing forward and to be the best version of myself. Thank you for your patience, understanding, and endless love.

To my family and friends, thank you for surrounding me with kindness, laughter, and a constant reminder that I am never alone. Your belief in me has fueled my passion to complete this work, and I couldn't have done it without you by my side. This book is a tribute to the power of community, family, and friendship, and I am so grateful for each of you.

Contents

Title Page
Copyright
Dedication
Introduction
Chapter 1: Understanding the Emotional Impact   1
Chapter 2: Legal Considerations   14
Chapter 3: Financial Planning and Stability   30
Chapter 4: Navigating Child Custody and Parenting Plans   45
Chapter 5: Finding Your Support System   63
Chapter 6: Self-Care and Mental Health   80
Chapter 7: Rebuilding Self-Esteem and Confidence   92
Chapter 8: Redefining Your Identity   106
Chapter 9: Co-Parenting Challenges and Solutions   119
Chapter 10: Legal Finalization and Moving   132

Forward	
Chapter 11: Long-Term Financial Planning	146
Chapter 12: Embracing New Beginnings	162
Epilogue	179
About The Author	181

Introduction

Divorce is one of life's most challenging transitions. It brings with it a whirlwind of emotions, questions, and uncertainties that can leave us feeling unprepared, overwhelmed, and alone. I know this because I've been there myself. When I went through my own divorce, I didn't have a clear guide, an easy process, or a reliable road map at my fingertips. Instead, I found myself piecing together bits of information, advice, and support from different places, struggling to make sense of it all. I wished there had been a comprehensive guide to help me understand what to expect, how to heal, and how to rebuild my life with strength and confidence.

This book is the guide I wish I'd had. It's here to offer you support, insights, and practical steps so that you don't have to navigate this journey alone. I wrote it to be both a comforting companion and a powerful resource for any woman going through the process of divorce. I hope that within these pages, you'll find clarity, strength, and inspiration to move forward.

Chapter 1: Understanding the Emotional Impact

THE STAGES OF GRIEF AND EMOTIONAL PROCESSING

Going through a divorce can feel emotionally overwhelming, and it often follows a process similar to the stages of grief. These stages represent common experiences, though they're not always linear, and people might move through them in different orders or revisit stages over time. Here's an outline of the typical stages, along with strategies for healing and moving forward:

1. Denial

Denial can be a coping mechanism that helps shield you from immediate pain. You might avoid thinking about the divorce, feel numb, or hold onto the hope of reconciliation. Allow yourself to feel your emotions rather than suppressing them. Writing in a journal or talking with supportive friends can help you process the reality of the situation.

2. Anger

Anger often surfaces as frustration over the loss, betrayal, or perceived injustices that led to the divorce. You may feel resentment toward your ex-partner or the circumstances. Find healthy outlets for your anger, such as exercising, venting in a journal, or talking with a therapist. Anger can be a motivating force for setting boundaries or making positive changes, but it's essential to manage it constructively.

3. Bargaining

This stage is often marked by "what if" thoughts and attempts to regain control. You might wonder if there was something you could have done differently or consider reuniting under certain conditions. Reflect on your thoughts and motivations. If you find yourself ruminating, remind yourself of the reasons for the divorce and focus on creating a vision for a healthier future.

4. Depression

Depression is often feelings of sadness, hopelessness, or even regret that can arise as the reality of the divorce sets in. Depression might make it hard to find joy or motivation, even in activities you once enjoyed. Seek support through therapy, support groups, or loved ones who can provide comfort and encouragement. Self-care activities, like exercising, meditating, or spending time in nature, can help improve mood gradually.

5. Acceptance

Acceptance is not necessarily "moving on" but coming to terms with the end of the marriage and beginning to envision life independently. In this stage, you can acknowledge the good and bad aspects of the relationship without feeling attached. Set personal goals and start investing time in new interests, friendships, and activities that bring joy and fulfillment. Acceptance is the foundation for building a new, fulfilling chapter in your life.

STRATEGIES TO OVERCOME

AND HEAL FROM DIVORCE

1. Allow Yourself to Grieve Fully: Let yourself feel the emotions without rushing to "get over it." Healing is gradual, and processing these feelings helps build resilience.

2. Lean on Support Networks: Friends, family, support groups, and therapists can provide empathy, perspective, and comfort. Sharing with others who understand what you're going through can be a huge source of strength.

3. Establish Healthy Boundaries: Limit communication with your ex where possible, especially if it's a source of stress or conflict. Boundaries help create the space you need to focus on your healing.

4. Reclaim Your Identity: Divorce can lead to a sense of lost identity. Rediscovering your hobbies, setting new goals, or trying out interests can help you reconnect with yourself.

5. Practice Self-Care: Physical and emotional well-being are interconnected. Engage in activities like exercising, journaling, meditation, or pursuing hobbies that nurture you.

6. Work with a Therapist or Coach: Therapists or coaches experienced in helping people navigate life transitions can help you work through emotions and create strategies for building a new future.

7. Take It One Day at a Time: Divorce recovery is a process, and setbacks are normal. Focus on taking small steps forward, and remind yourself that healing takes time.

Overcoming a divorce is challenging, but each stage of the process helps you gradually detach, heal, and begin to rebuild. In time, you can create a new life filled with purpose, joy, and a renewed sense of self.

RECOGNIZING AND VALIDATING YOUR FEELINGS

Recognizing and validating your feelings is a crucial part of emotional well-being, especially when going through challenging times. It involves acknowledging your emotions without judgment and allowing yourself to fully experience them. Here are steps on how to recognize and validate your feelings:

1. Pause and Reflect

Set aside a few minutes each day to check in with yourself. Ask, "How am I feeling right now?" and try to identify any emotions present, even if they seem subtle. Emotions often manifest physically. Tightness in the chest might signal anxiety, while tension in the jaw or fists can indicate anger. Recognizing these physical signs can help you identify underlying emotions.

2. Name Your Feelings

Rather than saying, "I feel bad," try to pinpoint the emotion, such as sadness, frustration, or disappointment. Expanding your emotional vocabulary can give you more clarity and control. Emotions like anger, jealousy, or sadness are often labeled as "bad," but they're normal and valuable parts of the human experience. Recognizing them without judgment is essential.

3. Allow Yourself to Feel Without Suppressing

Resist the urge to push away "negative" feelings or criticize yourself for feeling a certain way. Remember, emotions aren't inherently good or bad; they're signals that can guide you. Treat yourself with the same kindness you would offer a friend. If you're feeling overwhelmed, remind yourself that it's okay to feel this way and that the feeling will pass.

4. Express Your Feelings Constructively

Journaling can help clarify your emotions and release pent-up feelings. Write freely without worrying about structure or judgment. Sharing your emotions with a trusted friend, family member, or therapist can provide relief and perspective. Simply expressing how you feel can help validate and release the emotion.

5. Remind Yourself That Emotions Are Temporary

Instead of saying, "I am sad," try saying, "I am feeling sadness." This slight shift can help you see emotions as temporary experiences, rather than fixed parts of who you are. Mindfulness techniques, such as deep breathing or guided meditation, can help you observe your emotions without becoming overwhelmed by them. This can be particularly helpful in moments of intense feelings.

6. Reflect on the Causes of Your Emotions

Identifying what triggered your emotions can provide valuable insights. If you're feeling anxious, consider what events, thoughts, or situations may have contributed. While understanding your feelings is important, don't feel pressured to fully "solve" them. Sometimes, it's enough just to acknowledge that they're there.

BENEFITS OF RECOGNIZING AND VALIDATING YOUR FEELINGS

- **Improved Self-Awareness:** Knowing your emotions helps you understand yourself better and recognize your needs.
- **Enhanced Emotional Regulation:** Validating emotions reduces the tendency to suppress or intensify them, allowing you to manage your reactions more effectively.
- **Stronger Relationships:** Recognizing your emotions helps you communicate them more openly, improving connections with others.

Emotions are essential tools for understanding ourselves. By regularly recognizing and validating your feelings, you nurture a healthier, more compassionate relationship with yourself and build resilience for whatever life brings.

SEEKING EMOTIONAL SUPPORT

Seeking emotional support during a divorce can make a significant difference in your healing process, providing comfort, guidance, and a sense of community. Here's how to find and make the most of support resources like therapy, support groups, and other forms of assistance:

1. Consider Therapy for Individual Support

Look for a licensed therapist with experience in divorce, grief, or life transitions. They can help you process emotions, develop coping strategies, and work through any personal issues that arise.

Options for Therapy:

- **In-Person Therapy:** Many find comfort in face-to-face therapy for a more personal connection. Use local directories or websites like Psychology Today to find nearby professionals.
- **Online Therapy:** Platforms like BetterHelp or Talkspace allow you to connect with licensed therapists via video calls, chat, or messaging, which can be convenient if in-person visits feel overwhelming.

2. Join a Divorce Support Group

Support groups can provide a sense of community, reduce feelings of isolation, and offer shared perspectives. Talking with others who understand what you're going through can be both comforting and enlightening.

Find a Group:

- **In-Person Groups:** Many communities have in-person support groups for divorce. Check local community centers, churches, or counseling offices for resources.
- **Online Support Groups:** Websites like DivorceCare or Meetup offer online groups where people discuss their experiences and provide mutual support. These groups can be a lifeline, especially if you're not comfortable with in-person meetings yet.

3. Reach Out to Friends and Family

Select friends or family members who are empathetic listeners and nonjudgmental. Not everyone may understand what you're going through, so choose carefully to avoid unnecessary stress. Be honest about needing emotional support, whether that means just having someone to talk to or someone to help with day-to-day tasks. Letting people know how they can support you makes it easier for them to step up.

4. Use Self-Help Resources

Listening to experts discuss divorce and emotional resilience can provide a comforting perspective. There are many podcasts and blogs dedicated to navigating the challenges of divorce.

5. Practice Mindfulness and Self-Care Techniques

Techniques such as mindfulness meditation can help calm overwhelming feelings, increase self-awareness, and provide tools for managing stress. Apps like Headspace or Insight Timer have specific programs on grief and loss. Staying physically active can boost your mood and help release stress. Find activities that bring you joy, whether it's yoga, walking, or swimming.

6. Work with a Divorce Coach

A divorce coach is a professional who guides people through the divorce process, helping with emotional, practical, and even financial aspects. They're a great resource if you're looking for more tailored, holistic support. Many coaches offer virtual sessions. Look for a certified divorce coach or ask your therapist if they can recommend one.

7. Attend Workshops or Seminars

Many communities offer workshops that focus on specific topics like rebuilding self-esteem, co-parenting, or financial planning. These can provide practical advice while connecting you with others in a similar stage of life. If in-person options aren't available, many mental health and support organizations offer webinars on managing divorce stress and rebuilding.

8. Consider Financial and Legal Support Services

Financial stress often accompanies divorce, and financial counselors can help you plan for a new future. Having this guidance can alleviate a lot of worry, allowing you to focus on your emotional health. Working with a mediator or a lawyer focused on amicable resolutions can help reduce the emotional toll of legal disputes, making the transition smoother.

Tips for Making the Most of Support Resources:

- **Be Open and Honest:** Whether in therapy, a support group, or with friends, being honest about your emotions will allow you to receive the best support.

- **Set Boundaries:** Share only as much as you're comfortable with, and remember you have the right to stop conversations if they become overwhelming.
- **Take Your Time:** Healing is not a race. Permit yourself to move at your own pace.

Seeking support is a sign of strength, and surrounding yourself with compassionate resources can make the journey through divorce more manageable. With time, patience, and the right support, you'll find yourself growing stronger and ready to embrace new possibilities.

Chapter 2: Legal Considerations

UNDERSTANDING DIVORCE LAWS AND YOUR RIGHTS

Understanding divorce laws and your rights is essential for navigating the divorce process smoothly and protecting your interests. Here's a guide on how to get started:

1. Understand State-Specific Divorce Laws

Divorce laws vary widely by state, so check your state's specific requirements and guidelines. States differ in residency requirements, waiting periods, and grounds for divorce. States can allow for "no-fault" divorces (where neither party is blamed for the breakdown of the marriage) or "fault-based" divorces (where specific misconduct, such as adultery or cruelty, is cited). Know which applies to you, as it may affect the division of assets or custody.

2. Learn About Property Division

Distinguish Between Marital and Separate Property: Generally, "marital property" includes assets and debts acquired during the marriage, while "separate property" includes those acquired before the marriage or through inheritance or gifts. Understanding this distinction helps you know what's subject to division.

Community Property vs. Equitable Distribution: Some states (like California and Texas) follow "community property" laws, meaning marital assets are split 50/50. Most other states use "equitable distribution," where assets are divided fairly but not necessarily equally.

3. Understand Custody and Child Support Laws

Custody includes legal custody (the right to make major decisions) and physical custody (where the child lives). Custody arrangements can be joint or sole, depending on the best interests of the child. Child support is usually determined based on state guidelines that consider factors like parents' income, custody arrangements, and child needs. Familiarize yourself with these calculations to understand potential support obligations or entitlements.

4. Learn About Alimony (Spousal Support)

Alimony can vary in duration and amount. Some states offer temporary alimony during divorce proceedings, rehabilitative alimony (to support a spouse until they become self-sufficient), or permanent alimony. Courts consider factors like the length of the marriage, each spouse's financial situation, earning capacity, and contributions to the marriage. Knowing these factors can help you anticipate possible alimony obligations or entitlements.

5. Understand Your Rights to Retirement and Financial Accounts

Division of Retirement Assets: Retirement accounts (such as pensions or 401(k)s) may be considered marital property, and dividing them may require a Qualified Domestic Relations Order (QDRO). Know the implications for taxes and penalties when dividing retirement accounts.

Protect Your Financial Interests: Know how joint bank accounts, credit card debts, and other shared financial assets or liabilities are handled in your state. Keep records of all financial transactions and accounts to support your case.

6. Review Health Insurance and Benefits Rights

Understand COBRA Rights: If you were on your spouse's employer-sponsored health insurance, you may qualify for temporary coverage through COBRA. Check the duration and cost implications to avoid losing coverage.

Consider Life and Health Insurance Policies: Divorce may affect life insurance beneficiaries and health insurance coverage for any dependents. It's essential to review these policies and make updates as needed.

7. Know Your Rights in Mediation and Court

Many divorces are settled through mediation, which allows both parties to negotiate terms with a neutral third party. Mediation can be less costly and stressful than going to court. If mediation fails, your case may go to trial. Understand that a trial involves legal fees, court appearances, and possibly having a judge make decisions on your behalf.

8. Work with a Knowledgeable Divorce Attorney

Hire a Specialized Attorney: A divorce attorney can

provide personalized guidance, interpret state laws, and help protect your rights. Look for an attorney specializing in family law or divorce who is familiar with local judges and court procedures.

Ask Questions and Be Informed: Your attorney should explain all legal options, potential outcomes, and costs. Don't hesitate to ask questions and clarify any parts of the process that you don't understand.

9. Protect Your Financial and Legal Documents

Gather documentation of assets, debts, income, tax returns, and other financial records. These will be crucial during the property division and support calculation process. Ensure you have copies of marriage certificates, prenuptial agreements, estate plans, and other important legal documents. Having these accessible can simplify negotiations and ensure you know your rights.

10. Take Steps to Safeguard Your Rights

Avoid Making Rash Decisions: During a divorce, emotions can run high, and it may be tempting to make quick decisions to "get it over with." However, take your time to fully understand each choice's financial, legal, and emotional impact.

Plan for the Future: Update your will, power of attorney, and other legal documents once the divorce is finalized. Doing so ensures your assets and decisions align with your new circumstances.

ADDITIONAL TIPS

Use Online Resources: Websites like LegalZoom and your state's judicial website can offer guidance and provide forms.

Join Support Groups: Some groups focus on the legal and financial aspects of divorce and can offer personal insights and recommendations for local professionals.

By educating yourself on divorce laws, you'll feel more empowered and prepared to make decisions that align with your interests and future plans.

FINDING THE RIGHT ATTORNEY

Finding the right divorce attorney can make a significant difference in how smoothly your divorce process goes and how well your interests are represented. Here are some steps to help you find a suitable attorney:

1. Determine Your Divorce Needs

Consider the Complexity of Your Case: If your divorce is straightforward, with little property or no children involved, a general family lawyer may suffice. For more complex cases involving children, large assets, or disputes, you may need an attorney specializing in high-conflict or high-asset divorces.

Decide on Your Approach: If you want an amicable or collaborative divorce, look for an attorney skilled in mediation or collaborative law. If conflict is unavoidable, you might want an attorney with strong litigation experience.

2. Ask for Recommendations and Research Online

If you know people who have gone through a divorce, ask them about their experience with their attorney. Personal recommendations can help you find trustworthy professionals. Websites like Avvo, Martindale-Hubbell, and the American Academy of Matrimonial Lawyers (AAML) offer directories of divorce attorneys along with reviews and ratings. Reading reviews can help you understand other clients' experiences.

3. Verify Their Experience and Specialization

- **Confirm They Specialize in Family Law:** Divorce law is highly specialized, so ensure the attorney's primary focus is on family law or divorce cases.
- **Check Their Track Record:** Ask about the attorney's experience with cases similar to yours, especially if there are unique factors (e.g., child custody, business ownership, or international elements).

4. Schedule Initial Consultations

Meet with at least 2–3 attorneys to compare styles, fees, and strategies. Most attorneys offer initial consultations, sometimes free or for a reduced fee, where you can ask questions and gauge their compatibility with your case. Ask about their approach to cases, their experience with cases like yours, their thoughts on likely outcomes, and any additional support they can provide, like mediators or financial experts.

5. Ask Key Questions During Consultations

What's Your Experience with Cases Like Mine?: Find out if they have specific experience in issues relevant to your case, like custody, asset division, or high-conflict situations.

What is Your Communication Style and Availability?: Ask how frequently you'll get updates, their preferred communication methods, and how quickly they typically respond to emails or calls.

What Are Your Fees and Billing Structure?: Attorneys may bill by the hour, offer flat fees, or have retainer fees. Make sure you fully understand the costs and ask for an estimate based on your case's complexity.

6. Evaluate Compatibility and Trust

In my experience, some attorneys are very aggressive, while others focus on negotiation and settlement. Choose someone whose approach aligns with your values and goals. You'll need to share personal details with your attorney and rely on them for advice. If you feel uncomfortable, judged, or pressured, it may not be the right fit.

7. Look for Red Flags

Be cautious if an attorney guarantees specific outcomes, as divorce results depend on many factors. If they're slow to respond or hard to reach during your consultation period, they may be unresponsive later on. Avoid attorneys who are vague about costs, their approach, or anticipated challenges.

8. Consider Hiring a Collaborative or Mediation Attorney

Collaborative Law Attorneys: If you and your spouse are open to an amicable solution, a collaborative attorney can help you work together to reach an agreement without going to court.

Mediation Attorneys: Mediation attorneys focus on helping both parties come to an agreement and may save you time and money if you prefer a non-confrontational approach.

9. Verify Credentials and Licenses

You can look up most attorneys on your state bar's website to confirm their license and check for any disciplinary actions. Attorneys who belong to organizations like the AAML or the American Bar Association's Family Law Section may have additional expertise and dedication to family law.

10. Make Your Decision and Sign a Contract

Review Their Contract Carefully: Read through the engagement letter or contract to understand fees, services included, and what happens if you decide to switch attorneys. Clarify any uncertainties before signing.

Establish Clear Communication Guidelines: Set expectations for how often you'll get updates and the best ways to communicate with each other to keep your case on track.

Finding the right attorney for your divorce can make a significant impact on the outcome of your case and your overall experience. Take your time, do thorough research, and choose someone you trust to guide you through this challenging process.

PREPARING NECESSARY DOCUMENTATION

Preparing essential documents for a divorce can help streamline the process and protect your rights. Here's a list of the most important documents to gather:

1. **Personal Identification and Marriage Documentation**

- **Marriage Certificate:** Proof of your marriage is necessary to file for divorce.

- **Social Security Numbers:** These may be required for filing and any future financial paperwork.
- **Birth Certificates for Children:** These are needed for custody and support discussions.

2. Financial Statements

- **Recent Pay Stubs:** These show your current income, including bonuses or other benefits, and are needed for calculating child or spousal support.
- **Tax Returns (Last 3-5 Years):** Personal and business tax returns provide a record of your income, deductions, and financial situation over recent years.
- **Bank Statements (Last 6-12 Months):** Copies of checking and savings accounts show available assets and any recent transactions.

3. Property and Asset Documents

- **Real Estate Documents:** Include mortgage statements, deeds, property appraisals, and recent property tax assessments for any jointly or individually owned real estate.
- **Vehicle Titles and Loan Documents:** Gather titles, loan statements, and recent valuations for cars, boats, or recreational vehicles.

- **Retirement and Investment Accounts:** Collect statements for 401(k)s, IRAs, pensions, stocks, bonds, and mutual funds. You may need a Qualified Domestic Relations Order (QDRO) for certain retirement accounts.

4. Debts and Liabilities

- **Credit Card Statements:** Statements from joint or individual accounts over the past 6–12 months to document outstanding debt.
- **Loan Statements:** Mortgage loans, personal loans, student loans, or any other debts should be documented, including balances and monthly payment information.

5. Insurance Policies

- **Life Insurance:** Include policy details for term or whole life insurance, as well as beneficiary information and cash value (if applicable).
- **Health, Dental, and Vision Insurance:** Provide information on current health insurance policies for both spouses and dependents.
- **Homeowners or Renters Insurance:** Gather documents that list property covered under these policies.

6. Household and Personal Expenses

- **Monthly Budget and Expense Summary:** Outline typical monthly expenses for housing, utilities, food, child care, transportation, and personal expenses. This will help in determining support needs and living costs post-divorce.
- **Receipts or Statements for Major Purchases:** Documentation for significant household purchases, like appliances, furniture, or electronics, can help when dividing personal property.

7. Legal and Estate Documents

- **Wills and Trust Documents:** These are important if you or your spouse created wills or trusts during your marriage.
- **Power of Attorney and Healthcare Directives:** Any existing power of attorney or advance healthcare directives may need updating post-divorce.
- **Prenuptial or Postnuptial Agreements:** If you signed a prenuptial or postnuptial agreement, it's essential to have a copy for the divorce proceedings.

8. Documentation Related to Children

- **School and Extracurricular Records:** This includes report cards, tuition payments, and extracurricular activity expenses, which are relevant for custody and support.
- **Medical Records and Health Expenses:** Documentation of any ongoing medical care, prescriptions, or special needs expenses for children or dependents is essential for determining support.
- **Child Care and Daycare Costs:** Proof of daycare, after-school programs, or any childcare expenses.

9. Employment and Business Documents

- **Employment Contracts or Offer Letters:** Include details of current employment, job perks, or benefits.
- **Business Financials:** If you or your spouse owns a business, gather financial statements, profit and loss statements, and any ownership documents.
- **Stock Options or Bonuses:** Information on stock options, deferred compensation, bonuses, or incentive plans.

10. Proof of Ownership for Personal Property

- **Titles for Valuables:** For any assets like artwork, collectibles, jewelry, or family heirlooms, have documents showing ownership and recent valuations.
- **Appraisals:** If any high-value items have been appraised, include these appraisals as proof of worth.

Tips for Organizing and Protecting Documents:

- **Make Copies:** Create both physical and digital copies of all documents to ensure you have backup copies.
- **Store in a Secure Location:** Use a secure digital platform or lockbox to keep these documents safe and accessible.
- **Organize by Category:** Use folders for categories like finances, property, and child-related documents to keep everything organized.

Being prepared with these documents can help streamline the divorce process, reduce stress, and help you secure the best possible outcome.

Chapter 3: Financial Planning and Stability

ASSESSING YOUR FINANCIAL SITUATION

Assessing your financial situation during a divorce is crucial for understanding your current standing and preparing for your post-divorce life. Here's how to get started:

1. Document Your Income

Collect your pay stubs, ideally for the past 6–12 months, and tax returns for the past 2–3 years. This helps provide a full picture of your income, including any bonuses, commissions, or variable income sources. Document any additional income, such as rental income, side gigs, investments, alimony, or child support from a previous relationship, and any benefits like disability or social security.

2. List All Assets

Make an inventory of both marital (joint) and separate (individual) assets. Separate assets typically include anything you acquired before marriage or through inheritance/gifts, depending on your state's laws. List checking, savings, money market, and brokerage accounts, along with balances. For investment accounts, document retirement plans (401(k)s, IRAs, etc.), mutual funds, stocks, and bonds. Include details of any real estate properties, including your home, rental properties, vacation homes, or land, along with appraised values and mortgage balances. Document high-value items like vehicles, jewelry, collectibles, artwork, and electronics. Consider getting appraisals if the value is significant or disputed.

3. Review Debts and Liabilities

List all credit card accounts with outstanding balances, including any joint and individual cards. Document mortgages, car loans, student loans, and any personal loans, including amounts owed and monthly payments. Note any tax debts, medical bills, or other outstanding debts. This will give you a clear picture of what liabilities need to be addressed during the divorce.

4. Analyze Household and Personal Expenses

- **Create a Monthly Budget:** List your monthly expenses, including housing (rent/mortgage, utilities), groceries, transportation, insurance, child care, and entertainment. This helps you understand your typical cash flow and the minimum income you'll need post-divorce.
- **Account for Children's Expenses:** Include school tuition, extracurricular activities, clothing, and any other child-related costs. Courts often consider these expenses when determining child support.
- **Include Irregular Expenses:** List any non-monthly expenses, such as vehicle maintenance, home repairs, vacations, and health care costs. Knowing these helps you prepare for unpredictable costs in your post-divorce budget.

5. Assess Your Credit Standing

Obtain a free copy of your credit report from each major credit bureau (Experian, TransUnion, and Equifax). This helps you understand your credit health and identify any joint debt that could affect you post-divorce. Joint Debts like credit cards or loans will impact your credit score if your ex-spouse fails to pay. Consider refinancing or closing joint accounts where possible to protect your credit.

6. Estimate Future Financial Needs

Estimate if you'll need or receive alimony or child support, as these will affect your future income. Understanding these support obligations can help you budget for both current and future expenses. If you're entitled to a share of your spouse's retirement benefits, consult with a financial advisor to understand your options and ensure the division is handled correctly.

7. Evaluate Insurance Needs

- **Health Insurance:** If you're on your spouse's health insurance, check your options post-divorce, including COBRA or purchasing individual health coverage. Include estimated premiums in your budget.
- **Life Insurance and Beneficiaries:** Review any life insurance policies, and consider updating beneficiary designations to align with your new circumstances.

8. Work with Financial and Legal Advisors

- **Consult a Financial Advisor:** A financial advisor can help you understand the long-term effects of asset division, retirement, and support payments. They can also assist with budgeting for your post-divorce lifestyle.
- **Meet with a Divorce Attorney:** A divorce attorney can clarify how your state's laws impact asset division and alimony, helping you make informed decisions about your financial rights and obligations.

9. Create a Financial Plan for the Future

- **Draft a Post-Divorce Budget:** Based on your assessment, create a realistic budget for your post-divorce life. Include necessary expenses and any income adjustments to give yourself a clear view of your financial health.
- **Set New Financial Goals:** Identify short- and long-term goals, such as building an emergency fund, saving for a new home, or planning for retirement. This helps you stay focused and empowered as you navigate your new financial situation.

By taking a thorough, organized approach to your financial situation, you'll be better prepared to make informed decisions and secure a stable financial future.

BUDGETING AND FINANCIAL MANAGEMENT

Budgeting and managing finances during a divorce is essential for keeping control over your money and planning for a stable future. Here are steps to create a budget and manage your finances during this transition:

1. Assess Your Current Financial Situation

- **List All Income Sources:** Include your salary, freelance income, child support, alimony, and any other sources of income.
- **Document All Expenses:** Categorize monthly expenses, like housing, groceries, transportation, utilities, insurance, and debt payments, and consider occasional expenses like holidays and gifts.

- **Separate Joint Accounts:** If possible, start separating joint accounts to protect your finances. Close or remove yourself from shared credit cards or loans to avoid liability if your ex-partner uses them.

2. **Create a Temporary Budget**

- **Base it on Current Expenses and Income:** While in transition, use your current financial situation to create a budget for essential expenses and realistic spending limits.
- **Account for Legal and Divorce Expenses:** Set aside funds for legal fees, court costs, and any mediation or counseling fees. If you're unsure of exact costs, research averages or ask your attorney for an estimate.

3. **Prioritize Essential Expenses**

- **Cover the Basics First:** Ensure essential bills like rent, mortgage, utilities, and health insurance are fully funded.
- **Separate "Needs" from "Wants":** Focus on essential costs and reduce discretionary spending. This can help stretch your budget if your income changes post-divorce.

4. Plan for Independent Financial Responsibilities

Transition utilities, subscriptions, and bills to your name, if needed, and set up automatic payments to avoid missed payments. If you plan to move, include anticipated rent or mortgage expenses in your budget. Downsizing or temporarily moving in with family may be options to save on housing costs during this time.

5. Create a Post-Divorce Budget Plan

Consider any support payments you may receive or pay, and adjust for any job or income changes. Aim to save 3-6 months' worth of expenses. Having this buffer can help with unexpected costs and reduce stress as you adjust to new financial responsibilities.

6. Track Spending and Adjust as Needed

- **Use Budgeting Tools or Apps:** Apps like Mint, YNAB, or a simple spreadsheet can help you track spending and monitor cash flow.
- **Evaluate Your Progress Monthly:** Review your budget monthly to check if you're staying within limits or if adjustments are needed. Financial needs may change as you settle into post-divorce life, so keep your budget flexible.

7. Protect Your Credit and Financial Health

- **Monitor Your Credit Report:** Regularly review your credit report to ensure no joint accounts are impacting your credit score, and to catch any errors.
- **Avoid New Debt:** Focus on paying down existing debt rather than taking on new obligations. This will give you a cleaner financial slate and help you avoid interest expenses.

8. Set Financial Goals for the Future

Set goals like paying off debt, building savings, or eventually buying a home. Clear goals can keep you motivated and focused. Aim to replenish your savings and contribute to retirement accounts. If retirement funds were split in the divorce, meet with a financial advisor to adjust your retirement plans.

9. Seek Professional Financial Guidance

- **Consult a Financial Planner or Divorce Financial Advisor:** They can help you create a personalized plan that accounts for asset division, tax implications, and future financial health.
- **Consider a Credit Counselor if Needed:** If debt is a concern, a certified credit counselor can provide

debt management strategies and help you work out repayment options.

10. Stay Organized and Focused on Financial Stability

Save and organize statements, divorce-related expenses, and legal documents. These records can be helpful for taxes, refinancing, or credit applications. Adjusting to financial independence can take time. Maintain positive habits like saving, budgeting, and managing expenses to support your financial recovery and security. Building a financial foundation during and after divorce is a process, but by staying organized and proactive, you can set yourself up for stability and success in your new chapter.

ALIMONY, CHILD SUPPORT, AND DIVISION OF ASSETS

Managing or requesting alimony, child support, and asset division can be complex, but approaching these issues with preparation and understanding can help you advocate for your needs. Here are steps to take when handling each of these elements:

1. Requesting Alimony (Spousal Support)

- **Understand Alimony Types:** Alimony may be temporary, rehabilitative (to help you gain job skills or education), or permanent. Temporary alimony is often provided during the divorce process; rehabilitative and permanent alimony may be part of the final settlement.
- **Assess Eligibility:** Courts consider factors such as the length of the marriage, the standard of living during the marriage, each spouse's earning capacity, age, and health, as well as contributions to the marriage (like being a stay-at-home parent).
- **Document Financial Needs:** List monthly expenses, including housing, utilities, health insurance, childcare, and any career training costs, to show your financial needs post-divorce.
- **Provide Proof of Income and Assets:** You'll need to disclose income, assets, and debts to show your financial situation. Gather pay stubs, tax returns, and bank statements for this purpose.
- **Work with an Attorney:** A divorce attorney can help you request alimony and present a strong case, including arguing for the amount and duration you need.

2. Requesting Child Support

- **Learn State Guidelines:** Each state has child support guidelines based on income, custody arrangements, and other factors. These guidelines help ensure fair and consistent calculations.
- **Document Child-Related Expenses:** Create a detailed list of expenses, including health insurance, school fees, extracurricular activities, medical care, and daily living costs.
- **Gather Financial Documentation:** Provide income records for both you and your spouse. Courts will need pay stubs, tax returns, and any other proof of income (such as self-employment income).
- **Consider Custody Arrangements:** Child support calculations often depend on custody, including who has primary custody and how much time the child spends with each parent.
- **Request Adjustments if Needed:** If you or your spouse's income changes, or if there's a change in the child's needs (like increased medical or educational expenses), you can request a child support modification through the court.

3. Managing Division of Assets

Marital property, which is typically any asset acquired during the marriage, is generally subject to division. Separate property (assets owned before marriage or acquired by gift or inheritance) is typically retained by the original owner. Knowing the difference helps clarify what's to be divided. List all assets/debts and include real estate, bank accounts, retirement accounts, vehicles, investments, business interests, and personal property (like jewelry or valuable collections). Also, document all debts, including mortgages, car loans, and credit card balances.

Some states follow "equitable distribution" (assets are divided fairly, though not necessarily equally) while others are "community property" states (assets are split 50-50). Understand how your state's laws impact the division. Division of certain assets, like retirement accounts, may have tax consequences. For example, you may need a Qualified Domestic Relations Order (QDRO) to divide retirement funds without penalties. A financial advisor or tax professional can help evaluate tax implications. If possible, try mediation or collaborative divorce, where a neutral mediator helps both parties reach an agreement on asset division.

This can reduce legal costs and may lead to a more amicable solution.

4. Tips for Managing the Process

- **Work with a Divorce Attorney:** An experienced attorney can help you negotiate alimony, child support, and asset division to ensure your rights are protected. They can also provide guidance on fair settlements based on state laws.
- **Consider a Financial Advisor:** A divorce financial planner can help you understand the long-term impact of asset division, including retirement planning, tax implications, and investment management.
- **Stay Organized and Keep Detailed Records:** Maintain a file with all relevant financial documents, receipts, and any records of child-related expenses. Good documentation supports your case and ensures you have the necessary paperwork for negotiations.
- **Focus on Negotiation and Communication:** If possible, try to reach agreements through negotiation, especially on alimony and asset division. Open communication can lead to quicker, less contentious settlements, but be prepared for legal intervention if necessary.

Handling alimony, child support, and asset division can be challenging, but with the right support and preparation, you can work toward a settlement that secures your financial well-being and supports your future stability.

Chapter 4: Navigating Child Custody and Parenting Plans

UNDERSTANDING CUSTODY OPTIONS AND LEGAL TERMS

Understanding custody options and legal terms during a divorce is essential for making informed decisions about your children's future. Here's a guide to help you navigate this part of the process:

1. Learn the Types of Custody

- **Physical Custody:** Refers to where the child lives and who is responsible for day-to-day care. Physical custody can be sole (one parent has primary care and residence) or joint (both parents share significant time with the child).

- **Legal Custody:** Involves decision-making authority regarding major aspects of the child's life, such as education, health care, and religion. Legal custody can be sole (one parent makes decisions) or joint (both parents share decision-making).
- **Joint Custody:** Often divided into joint legal and/or joint physical custody. Joint legal custody is common, meaning both parents share in major decisions, even if one parent has more physical custody time.
- **Sole Custody:** One parent has both physical and legal custody, meaning they have the primary responsibility for the child's daily care and major decisions. The non-custodial parent may still have visitation rights, depending on the circumstances.

2. Understand Custody Arrangements and Parenting Time

- **Primary vs. Secondary Custody:** The parent who has the child most of the time is often referred to as the primary custodial parent. The other parent is typically the secondary custodial parent or non-custodial parent.
- **Visitation Rights:** Refers to the scheduled time

the non-custodial parent spends with the child. This can include regular weekly visits, extended time during holidays, or supervised visits if necessary.
- **Parenting Plan:** Many courts require a written parenting plan that outlines the custody arrangement, visitation schedule, and responsibilities. This plan ensures clarity and reduces conflicts by specifying each parent's roles.

3. Familiarize Yourself with Key Custody Terms

Courts prioritize what is best for the child when making custody decisions. This includes considering factors like the child's relationship with each parent, stability, safety, and each parent's ability to provide for the child's physical and emotional needs. After a custody order is in place, either parent may request a modification if there's a significant change in circumstances (e.g., relocation, job changes, or health issues).

Parental alienation refers to one parent's attempt to undermine or interfere with the child's relationship with the other parent. Courts generally discourage and may penalize attempts at alienation.

Mediation in many states requires mediation for custody issues. In mediation, a neutral third party helps parents negotiate custody terms without going to court. This approach can lead to a more cooperative arrangement.

4. Consider Custody Factors Courts Review

- **Stability and Continuity:** Courts often favor stability in the child's life, which may mean keeping them in their home or school whenever possible.
- **Parent-Child Relationship:** Courts evaluate the bond between each parent and the child, and they may consider the child's preferences if the child is old enough.
- **Parental Cooperation:** Courts consider each parent's willingness to support the child's relationship with the other parent. Collaborative parents may be more likely to be awarded joint custody.
- **Parental Ability and History:** This includes each parent's mental and physical health, history of caregiving, and any relevant issues like substance abuse, domestic violence, or neglect.

5. Understand Legal Processes for Custody

Courts often issue temporary custody orders while the divorce is ongoing. This arrangement can set a precedent for the final custody arrangement, so it's important to take it seriously. In cases where custody is highly contested, the court may order an evaluation by a mental health professional. This evaluation provides the court with insight into the family dynamics and the best arrangement for the child.

In some cases, a court may appoint a Guardian ad Litem (GAL), an advocate for the child's best interests. This person investigates the family situation and makes recommendations on custody and visitation.

6. Seek Legal Assistance

- **Consult a Family Law Attorney:** A qualified attorney can explain custody options, local laws, and help you prepare for court if needed.
- **Attend Parenting or Divorce Classes:** Some courts require parents to attend classes on co-parenting or child adjustment during divorce. These classes can provide strategies for supporting your child and understanding your legal obligations.

7. Create a Parenting Plan That Works for Your

Family

- **Specify Custody and Visitation Schedules:** Detail weekday, weekend, holiday, and summer schedules to avoid conflicts and provide stability for the child.
- **Address Communication and Decision-Making:** Include how you will communicate about the child's needs and make major decisions. Specify ways to handle disagreements to reduce conflict.
- **Adapt as Needed:** Parenting plans can be adjusted if both parents agree or by court modification if circumstances change. Flexibility is important, as children's needs evolve.

Understanding custody options and legal terms can help you approach this part of divorce with greater confidence. By working closely with a legal professional and focusing on your child's well-being, you can create a custody arrangement that supports stability, growth, and cooperation.

CO-PARENTING STRATEGIES

Co-parenting during a divorce can be challenging, but establishing clear strategies early on can help create a supportive, stable environment for your children. Here are some effective co-parenting strategies to consider:

1. Prioritize Open, Respectful Communication

Keep conversations focused on the children and stick to topics directly related to the children, such as schedules, health, education, and important events. Avoid discussing personal grievances. If face-to-face or phone conversations are challenging, consider using email or co-parenting apps like OurFamilyWizard or TalkingParents. These tools can help you manage schedules and keep track of important messages. Avoid heated conversations in front of your children, and set boundaries for when and where discussions about parenting will take place. Respect each other's time and privacy.

2. Create a Consistent Parenting Plan

- **Establish a Detailed Schedule:** Develop a clear visitation schedule that includes weekdays, weekends, holidays, and vacations. Consistency helps children feel secure and know what to expect.
- **Consider Your Children's Routine and Needs:** Try to maintain the children's routines as much

as possible, including school, activities, and bedtime, to minimize disruption.
- **Plan for Flexibility:** While consistency is important, allow for flexibility when necessary. Life events or emergencies may require adjustments, so work together to accommodate each other's needs if possible.

3. Respect Each Other's Parenting Style

Each parent may have different approaches to parenting, discipline, or household rules. Unless it's a safety concern, avoid criticizing or undermining the other parent's style. Present a united front for major decisions or family rules, discuss and agree on a unified approach. If both parents consistently enforce similar rules and values, it helps the children feel secure and reduces confusion. Avoid asking the children to choose between parents or sharing messages. Keep them out of adult discussions and decision-making processes.

4. Focus on the "Best Interests of the Child"

Whenever disagreements arise, frame your choices around what's best for the child's well-being, even if it requires compromise. Support each parent's relationship with the children and encourage your child to maintain a close bond with both parents. Avoid making negative comments about the other parent, as this can be confusing and hurtful for the child. Please be mindful of your child's emotions as children may feel sadness, confusion, or guilt during the divorce. Pay attention to their needs, offer reassurance, and consider counseling if they struggle to adjust.

5. Manage Transitions Smoothly

Aim for calm, friendly transitions during drop-offs and pick-ups. Avoid lengthy goodbyes or emotional displays, as these can increase anxiety for the child. Plan transitions around school or activities. If possible, schedule transitions at neutral locations, like school or a friend's house. This can make the process feel more routine and less emotionally charged.

Create a routine for packing essentials by ensuring the child has everything they need, like school items or favorite belongings, and communicate any needs to the other parent. A packing list or overnight bag can help.

6. Stay Positive and Encourage Stability

Children thrive on stability, so try to be consistent

in your actions, communication, and involvement. Focus on quality time with your child and make the most of your time by engaging in meaningful activities. Encourage positive memories and focus on quality rather than comparing time spent with each parent. Avoid Using Children as a Source of Information and don't ask children about the other parent's private life. Keep them out of adult issues and respect each other's personal boundaries.

7. Prepare for Big Decisions Together

Major decisions like school choice, medical care, or religious upbringing should ideally be made together. Regularly check in about long-term plans, educational goals, and any changes in the child's needs. If conflicts arise, consider a professional mediator or family therapist to help with decisions. Mediation can offer a neutral ground for resolving issues without escalating tension.

8. Take Care of Yourself, Too

- **Focus on Self-Care:** Co-parenting requires patience and resilience, so take time for self-care, rest, and stress-relieving activities.
- **Consider Counseling or Support Groups:** Support groups or therapy can provide emotional

guidance and help you process your feelings about the divorce. This can make you a more focused and positive co-parent.
- **Build a Support System:** Surround yourself with friends, family, or support networks to help manage stress. A strong support system can help you stay focused on providing the best for your children.

9. Be Patient as You Adjust

The transition to co-parenting is a process, and it may take time to find a rhythm that works well for everyone. Recognize progress and positive changes in your co-parenting relationship, even if they seem minor. These successes can build a foundation for a healthier dynamic.

10. Prioritize Your Child's Long-Term Well-being

Co-parenting is a partnership in raising your children. Focus on creating a stable, supportive environment instead of trying to control each other's actions. Ultimately, the goal of co-parenting is to raise well-adjusted, happy children. By working as a team and setting aside personal conflicts, you can both contribute to a healthier upbringing for your children.

Effective co-parenting takes commitment and cooperation, but over time, it can provide your children with a sense of security and love from both parents. By staying child-focused, communicating respectfully, and allowing space for compromise, you can create a positive co-parenting relationship that benefits everyone.

ENSURING THE WELL-BEING OF YOUR CHILDREN

Ensuring your children's well-being during a divorce is critical for their emotional stability and long-term resilience. Here are some strategies to help support and nurture them through this transition:

1. Communicate Openly and Reassure Them

Talk honestly in age-appropriate terms and explain the divorce in simple, clear language that fits their age and maturity level. Let them know they are not to blame and that both parents still love them. Remind them regularly that they are loved, safe, and will continue to have strong relationships with both parents. Assure them that they will be taken care of, even if some aspects of life are changing. Let them ask questions and express their feelings. Answer honestly but tactfully, and don't overburden them with adult-level details. Listening without judgment shows that their feelings matter.

2. Maintain Stability and Routine

A regular routine provides children with a sense of security. Establish a clear schedule for school, activities, and time with each parent, and try to maintain consistency. If possible, minimize changes in their daily lives, like switching schools or moving. Familiar routines and surroundings can be comforting during this uncertain time. Provide visual cues for the schedule. A shared calendar or app can help children understand where they'll be and when easing any anxieties about transitions.

3. Keep Conflict Away from the Children

- **Avoid Arguing in Front of Them:** Children should not witness parental conflicts, as they can cause stress and feelings of insecurity. Handle disagreements in private and approach co-parenting conversations calmly.
- **Protect Them from Negative Talk:** Avoid speaking negatively about the other parent in

front of your children. They need to feel they can love and trust both parents without feeling guilty or torn.
- **Don't Use Children as Messengers or Go-Betweens:** Communicate directly with the other parent, rather than asking your children to pass messages. This avoids placing them in uncomfortable or stressful situations.

4. Encourage Emotional Expression

Validate their feelings and let them know it's okay to feel sad, angry, or confused about the divorce. Encourage them to express their emotions in a safe environment without judgment.

Teach healthy coping mechanisms by showing them ways to process emotions constructively, such as talking to trusted adults, journaling, or engaging in activities they enjoy.

Consider counseling if needed by a family therapist or counselor specializing in divorce can provide children with a safe space to explore their feelings, especially if they are struggling to cope.

5. Support Their Relationship with Both Parents

- **Encourage Positive Relationships with Both**

Parents: Children benefit from close relationships with both parents. Support their time with the other parent, even if it's difficult for you.
- **Facilitate Communication:** Allow and encourage regular phone calls, video chats, or letters with the other parent when they're apart. This helps maintain a sense of connection and stability.
- **Respect Parenting Time:** Be consistent with custody schedules and don't withhold visitation as a form of punishment. Honor the time children have with each parent, showing that both relationships are valued.

6. Be Attentive to Changes in Behavior or Mood

Divorce can affect children in various ways. Look for changes in behavior, sleep, appetite, academic performance, or social interactions that might indicate they're struggling. If you notice concerning changes, reach out to teachers, counselors, or mental health professionals. Early intervention can help them navigate these feelings before they become more serious.

Take time to ask how they're doing. Consistent conversations provide opportunities for children to share thoughts or worries they may otherwise keep hidden.

7. Spend Quality Time with Each Child

- **Focus on Quality, Not Just Quantity:** Dedicate uninterrupted time to bond, listen, and engage in activities they enjoy. This one-on-one attention can provide comfort and show that you're there for them.
- **Stay Involved in Their Activities:** Attend school events, sports, or hobbies they're passionate about. Continuing these activities shows that, despite the changes, your involvement in their life remains steady.
- **Create New Traditions:** Building positive memories with new traditions—like movie nights, weekend hikes, or special outings—can help redefine family time in a supportive way.

8. Model Resilience and Positivity

Children take emotional cues from their parents. Try to manage your own emotions constructively and show resilience, which can help them feel secure and hopeful. Focus on solutions rather than problems by showing your children that challenges can be managed and overcome. Focusing on positive aspects (like spending special time together) helps create an optimistic outlook.

Take care of yourself as your emotional and physical well-being influences theirs. Taking time to care for yourself through healthy habits, therapy, or support groups allows you to be a calmer, more present parent.

9. Prepare for Big Changes Together

Communicate major changes ahead of time to give your children time to adjust to upcoming changes, such as moving homes or new living arrangements. Explain the changes, and involve them in parts of the process to give them some control. Plan for smooth transitions if there are significant transitions, such as switching between households, and plan in ways that minimize stress, like scheduling transitions around neutral times (e.g., before or after school). Allow time for adjustment and understand that children may take time to adapt to new routines or living situations. Be patient and offer support as they gradually settle into these changes.

10. Seek Professional Help When Necessary

- **Consider Family Therapy:** Family counseling can support communication, help address the specific needs of each child, and provide coping

strategies for the entire family.
- **Encourage Individual Counseling for Children:** If a child seems particularly affected, a therapist can provide them with tools to manage feelings healthily and gain confidence in expressing their needs.
- **Use Co-Parenting Classes:** Some communities offer co-parenting classes, which teach strategies for navigating divorce while focusing on children's well-being.

Supporting your children through a divorce requires consistency, compassion, and reassurance. By maintaining open communication, preserving stability, and fostering a cooperative environment with your co-parent, you can help your children feel secure and loved as they adjust to the changes.

Chapter 5: Finding Your Support System

LEANING ON FAMILY AND FRIENDS

Leaning on friends and family during and after a divorce is essential because their support can help you navigate the emotional, practical, and mental challenges of this major life change. Here are some reasons why a strong support system is so beneficial during this time:

1. Emotional Support and Comfort

Friends and family can be safe, non-judgmental listeners, offering an outlet for you to express emotions like sadness, anger, or confusion. Talking openly about your feelings with loved ones can reduce the weight of these emotions. Divorce can feel isolating, but knowing that people are there for you can offer comfort and reassurance, helping you avoid feelings of loneliness. Loved ones can remind you of your strengths, celebrate your progress, and encourage you when you're feeling uncertain. Having people who believe in you can make a big difference in maintaining self-confidence during difficult times.

2. Perspective and Guidance

Friends and family can offer insights and advice from an outside perspective, helping you see situations more clearly when emotions are running high. Divorce involves many decisions about legal, financial, and personal matters. Trusted people can offer helpful feedback as you weigh your choices, helping you make more grounded decisions. If loved ones have been through similar situations, they may offer advice or strategies that helped them. Learning from others' experiences can provide comfort and give you practical ways to cope.

3. Practical Support and Assistance

Divorce often disrupts daily routines. Family and friends can assist with practical tasks, like helping with childcare, running errands, or cooking meals, especially during high-stress periods. Trusted people may have insights or even professional connections (like attorneys or financial advisors) that could be helpful. They may also help you organize paperwork or manage other essential tasks. If you're in the process of moving or need a place to stay temporarily, friends and family can provide that physical support, giving you the stability and comfort of a home environment during a challenging time.

4. Encouragement to Heal and Move Forward

Loved ones can remind you to take care of yourself, encouraging healthy habits like exercise, rest, and socializing. They can also help you find joy in small activities that bring a sense of normalcy and positivity. Friends and family can invite you to social activities or help you try new experiences, providing opportunities to reconnect with life outside of the divorce. Social support and positive distractions are essential for recovery. Loved ones can help you embrace this new chapter, encouraging you to rediscover hobbies, pursue new goals, and rebuild your life with confidence. Their belief in you can help you see the potential for growth and renewal.

5. A Source of Accountability

Friends and family can provide gentle accountability, encouraging you to maintain boundaries and avoid unhealthy communication with your ex-partner. This is important for focusing on healing and moving forward. By regularly checking in, friends and family can help you avoid withdrawing socially, which can lead to feelings of depression. Having a network of people who care keeps you connected and engaged. They can help you stay accountable to self-care routines, from therapy appointments to wellness practices, which are crucial for long-term healing.

6. Emotional Stability for Children

If you have children, friends and family can provide emotional support to them as well, helping them process the transition. Extended family or close friends can offer children continuity, stability, and an additional sense of security. Divorce can make scheduling complicated. Trusted family members or friends can assist with child care, helping maintain consistency in routines and providing familiar, comforting environments. Supportive family members can model positive relationships and resilience, showing your children how to handle challenges healthily.

By leaning on friends and family, you gain a powerful support system that helps you cope, grow, and rebuild after divorce. Their empathy, encouragement, and assistance can make the journey smoother, empowering you to navigate this new chapter with resilience and confidence.

JOINING SUPPORT GROUPS

Joining a support group during and after a divorce can offer immense benefits, providing emotional, practical, and social support tailored specifically to the challenges of this life transition. Here's why joining a divorce support group can be incredibly valuable:

1. Emotional Validation and Understanding

- **Connect with People Who "Get It":** Divorce support groups are filled with people who are experiencing similar emotions and situations. This shared understanding fosters a safe space where members can talk openly without fear of judgment.
- **Feel Less Isolated:** Divorce can be lonely,

especially if you feel like others in your life can't fully understand what you're going through. A support group offers companionship and reassurance, helping you feel less alone.
- **Gain Emotional Validation:** Group members are often at different stages of the divorce process, which means there's always someone who can relate to what you're feeling. This validation helps normalize your emotions and reduces feelings of shame or self-doubt.

2. Healthy Processing of Emotions

Support groups encourage open sharing, allowing you to process emotions like sadness, anger, guilt, and grief in a healthy way. Expressing emotions in this setting can be more constructive than bottling them up. Group facilitators and members often share techniques to manage stress, cope with sadness, and handle complex emotions. These shared strategies can be effective for healthily processing feelings. Being around others who are actively working through similar emotions can help minimize feelings of anger or resentment, fostering a more positive and balanced outlook.

3. Practical Advice and Problem-Solving

- **Receive Advice on Legal and Financial Matters:** Members often share practical tips and resources, like finding a good attorney, understanding custody agreements, or managing finances post-divorce. This collective wisdom can be very helpful.
- **Gain Perspective on Life Changes:** Group members often provide insight into navigating various post-divorce adjustments, from co-parenting and moving to dating again. Learning from others' experiences can make these transitions smoother.
- **Find Solutions to Common Challenges:** Support groups often discuss typical issues that arise during and after divorce, offering actionable solutions that you can adapt to your situation.

4. Positive Accountability and Motivation

- **Set and Achieve Personal Goals:** Support groups often encourage members to set personal goals, whether they relate to emotional healing, career development, or self-care. The group can help hold you accountable and celebrate your progress.
- **Encouragement to Keep Moving Forward:**

Members of support groups frequently motivate each other, pushing you to take positive steps forward, even when it feels challenging. This encouragement fosters resilience and progress.

- **Develop Healthy Habits:** Many groups emphasize the importance of self-care practices like exercise, meditation, and therapy. The group can motivate you to stay committed to these practices, promoting your emotional and physical well-being.

5. Learn Coping Skills for Co-Parenting and Family Dynamics

Gain Co-Parenting Tips for those with children, support groups often discuss co-parenting strategies, allowing you to learn how others manage shared custody and communicate with ex-partners. Divorce can impact extended family and friendships. Group members often discuss navigating these changes, sharing how they've handled difficult conversations or rebuilt support networks. Group members frequently share tips on helping children adjust, offering insights on how to protect their well-being and minimize stress during the transition.

6. Develop New Social Connections

Expand your support network as support groups can be a wonderful way to meet new people, including those who become close friends. These connections can be instrumental as you rebuild your life post-divorce. Especially if you're not ready to start dating again or feel uncomfortable in traditional social settings, support groups provide a social outlet that's rooted in mutual respect and understanding. Many support groups plan social activities or outings, which provide fun, stress-free ways to engage with others and begin enjoying life outside the context of the divorce.

7. Encouragement to Focus on Self-Growth and Healing

Promote personal growth and self-reflection as divorce support groups often encourage you to reflect on your needs, goals, and identity beyond the marriage. This can be empowering, helping you rediscover your strengths and passions. Being part of a group where others are working to rebuild their lives can inspire hope and resilience. Seeing others overcome challenges helps remind you that healing and growth are possible. Support groups help members turn the page on their divorce and begin envisioning a positive future. Through shared goals and encouragement, the group can help you develop a hopeful mindset as you look forward.

8. Reduced Risk of Depression and Anxiety

Divorce can increase the risk of depression or anxiety due to the social and emotional changes involved. A support group can prevent these feelings from intensifying by providing regular, meaningful interaction. Many support groups emphasize mental wellness, and teaching skills for managing stress and anxiety, such as mindfulness or grounding exercises, which can be particularly helpful during this period. When you see others finding ways to rebuild and thrive, it reinforces the idea that there is life—and happiness—beyond divorce. This hope can be essential in combating depression and cultivating a sense of purpose.

By joining a support group, you can find understanding, advice, and encouragement to help you navigate your emotions and rebuild your life after divorce. These groups offer a unique, empathetic environment that can provide comfort and direction when you need it most.

BUILDING A NETWORK OF RESOURCES

Building a network of resources during and after a divorce is essential for emotional support, practical assistance, and long-term stability. A strong network can help you navigate the complexities of divorce and empower you as you rebuild your life. Here's how to create and leverage a reliable network of resources:

1. Identify Key Professionals

Finding an experienced divorce attorney is crucial for understanding your legal rights, protecting your interests, and navigating the divorce process. Seek recommendations, research local attorneys, and consider meeting with a few to find one who aligns with your needs. Divorce often brings financial changes. A financial advisor can help you assess your finances, plan for your future, and make informed decisions about assets, alimony, and budgeting. A mental health professional can provide emotional support, helping you process your emotions, build resilience, and focus on personal growth. Therapists with expertise in divorce recovery can be especially helpful. If you need to buy, sell, or rent a property, a knowledgeable real estate agent can guide you through your options, helping you make housing decisions that align with your post-divorce life.

2. Connect with Local Support Groups

Local and online divorce support groups offer a community of people going through similar experiences. They can provide emotional support, practical advice, and social connections. Some groups also provide referrals for professionals like therapists and financial advisors. Many communities offer co-parenting classes or workshops, which can provide valuable skills, resources, and networking opportunities with other co-parents. Nonprofit organizations, community centers, and churches often host programs for individuals going through divorce. These programs may offer support groups, counseling, and referrals to local resources.

3. Develop Relationships with Trusted Friends and Family

Lean on supportive friends and family members to cultivate relationships with people who offer emotional stability and encouragement. They can provide practical assistance, offer advice, and be a sounding board for decisions. Sometimes, different people are better suited to different forms of support. For example, one friend might be a great listener, while another might help with logistical support like childcare or household tasks. Reach out to people who might be going through or have gone through similar experiences. This shared understanding can be particularly comforting, and they may also introduce you to helpful resources.

4. Use Online Resources and Communities

Many online communities and forums offer resources, support, and advice from people who have been through divorce. They can help learn about the process, receive emotional support, and access recommendations. Facebook groups or LinkedIn communities focused on divorce or life transitions can be valuable. You may find suggestions for attorneys, financial advisors, therapists, or even practical tips on handling paperwork.

Access educational websites like DivorceNet, LegalZoom, or government resources that offer information about divorce law, finances, and parenting. These platforms can help you understand your rights and find tools for managing the legal aspects of divorce.

5. Seek Out Professional Organizations and Networks

- **Join Divorce-Focused Nonprofits and Organizations:** Groups like the Association of Divorce Financial Planners (ADFP) or Second Saturday (a divorce workshop series) offer guidance on navigating finances, parenting, and legal matters.
- **Consider Industry-Specific Networks:** If your job is affected by the divorce, explore professional organizations or career coaches for support and resources related to employment, career growth, or workplace adjustments.
- **Build a Legal Support Network:** If you need additional legal help (like advice on child custody or estate planning), ask your divorce attorney for referrals to other legal professionals or organizations that can assist you.

6. Explore Financial Resources and Assistance Programs

Many financial institutions and community centers offer workshops on budgeting, investing, and retirement planning. These can be invaluable as you adjust to new financial realities. Government and nonprofit programs offer financial assistance, food support, and housing resources for those in transition. Look into local programs that support single-parent households. Credit counseling services provide advice on managing debt, building credit, and creating a realistic financial plan.

7. Create a Go-To List of Health and Wellness Resources

- **Compile Mental Health Resources:** Include therapists, support groups, and crisis hotlines in your network for moments when you need extra support. Consider virtual therapy options if you prefer remote sessions.
- **Stay Active with Wellness Groups:** Physical activity can reduce stress and improve well-being. Join a yoga class, hiking group, or gym, or look for wellness programs in your community that offer holistic support.
- **Prioritize Self-Care:** Include resources for activities that boost mental and emotional health, like meditation apps, journaling groups, and hobby clubs. Self-care helps you stay balanced and focused.

8. Consider Rebuilding Your Professional Network

Divorce can sometimes impact professional life. Maintaining relationships with colleagues and mentors provides a network of career support and can be helpful if you consider changing jobs or advancing your career. Industry-specific associations can offer career guidance, job opportunities, and resources to support you in professional growth, which can be empowering during a period of personal change. If divorce changes your financial landscape, you may want to build new skills. Many communities and online platforms offer training programs that can increase job opportunities.

9. Establish Parenting Resources if You Have Children

Find parenting support groups focused on single parenting or co-parenting. They offer guidance on managing parenting challenges and provide emotional support. For single parents, reliable childcare and educational support are essential. Connect with local schools, community centers, and parenting networks to find trusted options. Children benefit from support as they process the divorce. Find a counselor or therapist who specializes in family or child therapy to help them adapt and develop healthy coping mechanisms.

10. Regularly Re-Evaluate and Update Your Resource Network

Adapt to new needs and life phases as you move through and past divorce, your needs may change. Continually assess whether you need new support, like a financial planner for long-term goals or a career coach if you're entering a new field.

Stay in touch with trusted contacts as maintaining connections with attorneys, therapists, or financial advisors can be valuable in the future, whether for ongoing support or advice as circumstances change. Diversify your network by including people and resources from different aspects of life, such as work, family, hobbies, and self-care. A broad network provides a balanced foundation for recovery and growth.

Creating a network of resources gives you the support, knowledge, and stability you need during and after divorce. These resources can help you regain confidence, rebuild your life, and navigate this challenging transition with resilience and optimism.

Chapter 6: Self-Care and Mental Health

IMPORTANCE OF SELF-CARE ROUTINES

Self-care routines during a divorce are essential for maintaining your mental, emotional, and physical health through an extremely stressful time. Divorce brings a unique set of challenges, and without self-care, it's easy to feel overwhelmed and depleted. Here's why self-care is so important during this period:

1. Helps Manage Emotional Stress

Divorce often brings a flood of emotions, including sadness, anger, anxiety, and sometimes relief. Self-care routines like journaling, therapy, or meditation help you healthily process these feelings. Taking time for yourself fosters resilience, which helps you navigate the ups and downs with a stronger mindset. Self-care helps create a calm center to return to, even during the toughest days.

2. Supports Physical Health and Energy Levels

The stress from divorce can take a toll on your body, impacting sleep, energy, and even immune health. Self-care routines like exercise, healthy eating, and good sleep hygiene counteract these effects, helping you stay strong. Self-care helps you recharge, making it easier to handle daily responsibilities and focus on the decisions you need to make.

3. Provides Mental Clarity and Focus

Divorce requires many critical decisions, from finances to custody. Self-care practices like mindfulness or quiet time help clear your mind, so you can make choices from a place of calm, not chaos. Regular self-care prevents burnout, which can lead to feelings of mental overload. This allows you to stay more organized and focused on each step forward.

4. Boosts Self-Worth and Identity

Divorce can shake your sense of identity, especially

if you've been in a long-term relationship. Self-care lets you reconnect with who you are as an individual, rediscover your passions, and strengthen your self-worth. By dedicating time to your well-being, you reinforce that you deserve care and attention. This can be incredibly empowering, reminding you that you are enough on your own.

5. Creates Stability and Routine

Divorce can feel like a loss of control, but having a daily or weekly self-care routine gives you a healthy foundation to rely on. Regular self-care acts as an anchor, offering a bit of normalcy and comfort even when life feels turned upside down.

6. Promotes Long-Term Healing

Self-care builds a habit of prioritizing yourself, which can positively shape your life beyond divorce. A strong self-care foundation allows you to approach future relationships from a place of strength and independence, ensuring you're healthy and fulfilled on your own first.

Self-care during a divorce is not just about surviving the process but about growing through it. It allows you to rebuild from a place of strength, ultimately helping you heal, regain confidence, and look forward to a fulfilling future.

STRATEGIES FOR STRESS MANAGEMENT

Managing stress during a divorce is crucial for maintaining your mental, emotional, and physical well-being. Here are some effective strategies to help you stay balanced and resilient:

1. Establish a Self-Care Routine

- **Exercise Regularly:** Physical activity helps relieve stress and improves mood by releasing endorphins. Try yoga, walking, or any activity you enjoy.
- **Prioritize Sleep:** Quality sleep is essential for emotional stability. Develop a relaxing pre-sleep routine, such as reading or practicing deep breathing.
- **Eat Nutrient-Rich Foods:** Eating well-balanced meals can stabilize your energy and mood, helping you feel more in control.

2. Practice Mindfulness and Meditation

- **Meditate Daily:** Even a few minutes of

meditation can reduce stress, allowing you to approach challenges calmly.
- **Focus on Deep Breathing:** During moments of high stress, practice slow, deep breaths to calm your nervous system. This can help prevent anxiety from taking over.
- **Stay Present:** Focus on one day at a time to avoid feeling overwhelmed by thinking too far ahead.

3. Set Healthy Boundaries with Your Ex-Partner

- **Limit Communication to Essentials:** Minimize contact if it reduces stress, and keep conversations focused on necessary topics like finances or child custody.
- **Use Neutral Channels if Needed:** If conversations become tense, use email or co-parenting apps to communicate more constructively.
- **Establish Boundaries Around Emotional Topics:** Protect your mental health by avoiding emotionally charged discussions that don't contribute to resolution.

4. Seek Support from Loved Ones and Professionals

- **Lean on Friends and Family:** Talking with trusted people can ease feelings of isolation. They can provide comfort, distraction, or a listening ear.

- **Consider Joining a Support Group:** Divorce support groups offer shared experiences and coping ideas, reminding you that you're not alone.
- **Work with a Therapist:** Therapy offers a safe space to process feelings and develop healthy coping strategies.

5. Stay Organized with Legal and Financial Tasks

- **Create a To-Do List:** Dividing tasks into manageable steps can reduce feelings of being overwhelmed. Prioritize tasks, so you focus on one thing at a time.
- **Document Everything:** Keep organized records of finances, custody arrangements, and communications to reduce future stress.
- **Hire a Competent Attorney:** Having a knowledgeable attorney you trust can ease your burden, allowing you to focus on healing.

6. Give Yourself Time for Relaxation and Fun

- **Engage in Hobbies:** Spend time doing activities you enjoy, like painting, cooking, or sports, to bring positivity and relaxation into your routine.
- **Schedule "Me Time":** Dedicate time each week to relax, whether it's a spa day at home, reading a

favorite book, or watching a movie.
- **Practice Gratitude:** Keep a journal of small, positive moments each day, which can help you stay grounded and focused on what's going well.

7. Develop a New Daily Routine

- **Create Structure:** Structure can help reduce stress by providing a sense of stability. Plan daily routines that include self-care, work, and social time.
- **Set Small Goals:** Break your day into achievable goals to keep you motivated and focused on progress.
- **Celebrate Small Wins:** Acknowledge each step forward, no matter how small, to maintain momentum and foster a positive mindset.

8. Give Yourself Permission to Feel and Process Emotions

- **Don't Rush the Healing Process:** Allow yourself to feel the emotions that come up without judging yourself. Take each day as it comes.
- **Journal Regularly:** Writing out your thoughts can help you process and release emotions, which reduces stress over time.
- **Practice Self-Compassion:** Treat yourself with

the kindness you would show a friend. Remind yourself that healing takes time, and it's okay to have difficult days.

9. Engage in Mindful Physical Activities

- **Try Yoga or Tai Chi:** These practices combine movement with mindfulness, helping you center yourself while relieving stress.
- **Get Outdoors:** Spending time in nature can be grounding and help clear your mind.
- **Try Breathing Exercises:** Deep breathing exercises can be calming and easy to do whenever stress arises.

10. Focus on the Future and Build a Vision for What's Next

- **Set Personal Goals:** Focus on areas of growth, whether that's in career, health, or hobbies, to remind yourself that there's a fulfilling future ahead.
- **Create a Vision Board:** Visualizing a positive future can bring hope and motivation to move forward with purpose.
- **Reframe the Experience as a New Beginning:** Embrace the opportunity to rediscover yourself, set new priorities, and design a life that feels

fulfilling.

Incorporating these strategies into your daily life can help make the divorce process less overwhelming and more manageable, building a foundation of strength and resilience as you move forward.

SEEKING PROFESSIONAL MENTAL HEALTH SUPPORT

Seeking professional mental health support during a divorce is crucial because divorce is one of the most emotionally challenging life events, often bringing intense feelings of sadness, anxiety, anger, and loss. Here's why working with a mental health professional can be so beneficial during this time:

1. Safe Space for Emotional Processing

A therapist offers non-judgmental, neutral support that can be hard to find elsewhere. They provide a safe space to openly discuss painful or confusing emotions. Divorce can bring up emotions that feel overwhelming. Therapy allows you to express these feelings in a structured way, helping you process grief, anger, or guilt.

2. Tools for Managing Stress and Anxiety

Therapists teach coping techniques to manage stress and anxiety, such as mindfulness or deep breathing, which can be invaluable during high-stress periods. The stress of divorce often leads to anxiety or depression, and a mental health professional can help manage or prevent these through personalized strategies and, when necessary, therapy.

3. Help with Decision-Making and Clarity

A therapist can help you approach decisions—like custody, finances, or communication with your ex—from a calm, logical perspective instead of one clouded by strong emotions. Therapy can help you understand your reactions, boundaries, and needs, providing clarity on what matters most to you as you plan your next steps.

4. Support in Building Self-Esteem and Identity

Divorce often affects self-esteem, especially if it impacts your sense of identity. Therapy helps you reconnect with your values, strengths, and goals, restoring a positive self-image. Working with a therapist allows you to explore your individuality outside of marriage, supporting personal growth and helping you rediscover who you are as an independent person.

5. Improved Communication and Co-Parenting Skills

Divorce can involve tense interactions with an ex-partner. Therapy can teach communication strategies that reduce conflict and help you communicate respectfully, especially in co-parenting situations. For parents, therapy provides tools for creating a healthy, cooperative co-parenting relationship, which is essential for children's well-being.

6. Long-Term Resilience and Healing

Prevent long-term emotional scars by healthily working through emotions. Therapy can reduce the risk of long-lasting resentment, anger, or sadness. Therapy helps you work through issues to develop a deeper self-understanding, which benefits future relationships by building healthier patterns.

7. Personalized Support for Unique Challenges

Everyone's experience of divorce is unique, and therapy can provide tailored support based on your individual challenges, such as managing finances alone or dealing with shared social circles. As you transition from married to single life, therapy helps you adapt to the ongoing changes in a way that promotes your well-being.

8. Enhanced Support for Your Children

Maintaining your mental health supports your ability to provide a stable, reassuring environment for your children, which is especially important during a family change. Seeking help shows your children that it's okay to ask for support when facing difficulties, which can positively impact their resilience and coping skills.

Therapy during a divorce is an investment in yourself, providing a foundation for healing, resilience, and positive growth. It helps you navigate the immediate challenges and prepares you for a brighter, healthier future.

Chapter 7: Rebuilding Self-Esteem and Confidence

OVERCOMING NEGATIVE SELF-TALK

Overcoming negative self-talk during a divorce is essential for maintaining self-confidence, emotional stability, and a hopeful outlook. Here are some strategies to help you shift away from critical thoughts and build a more positive mindset:

1. Acknowledge and Challenge Negative Thoughts

- **Identify Patterns:** Notice when you engage in negative self-talk, such as thoughts like "I'll never be happy" or "I'm a failure." Awareness is the first step toward change.
- **Challenge the Validity:** Ask yourself if these

thoughts are truly accurate or if they're exaggerated by emotions. Reframe thoughts in a more balanced, factual way. For instance, change "I'll never be happy" to "This is a hard time, but I'm taking steps to move forward."

2. Practice Self-Compassion

- **Treat Yourself Like a Friend:** Imagine what you would say to a friend going through a divorce. You'd likely be kind and supportive, not judgmental. Show yourself the same kindness.
- **Acknowledge Effort, Not Perfection:** Remind yourself that healing takes time and that you're doing the best you can. Celebrate small steps forward, no matter how minor.

3. Reframe "Failure" as Learning

- **Focus on Growth:** Shift your perspective from seeing the divorce as a failure to viewing it as an opportunity for growth and self-discovery.
- **List Positive Takeaways:** Consider what you've learned about yourself and your needs through this process. Recognize any new strengths or insights that have come from the experience.

4. Use Positive Affirmations

- **Set Daily Affirmations:** Replace negative thoughts with affirmations like, "I am worthy of love," "I am capable of creating a happy future," or "I am stronger every day."
- **Write Affirmations Where You'll See Them:** Place sticky notes with affirmations on your mirror, in your journal, or in places you'll encounter throughout the day to reinforce a positive mindset.

5. Shift Focus to the Present

- **Mindfulness Techniques:** Practice staying present rather than dwelling on the past or fearing the future. Use deep breathing or grounding exercises when you feel overwhelmed by negative thoughts.
- **Celebrate Small Wins:** Focus on small, positive actions you can take today, like making a healthy meal, going for a walk, or reaching out to a friend.

6. Journal to Reflect and Release

- **Challenge Negative Beliefs:** Write down negative thoughts and counter them with facts or positive perspectives. For example, if you write "I'm unlovable," counter it with "I have friends and

family who love and support me."
- **Express Gratitude:** Include a few things you're grateful for each day. This simple practice can reframe your mindset and reduce the power of negative self-talk.

7. Limit Comparisons to Others

- **Focus on Your Journey:** Comparing your situation to others can fuel negativity. Remind yourself that everyone's journey is unique and that you are on your path to healing.
- **Take Breaks from Social Media:** Social media can make it easy to compare yourself to others, so take breaks if it increases your negative self-talk. Focus on real-life connections instead.

8. Seek Support from Loved Ones or a Therapist

- **Share Your Feelings:** Talking with trusted friends or family members can help you gain perspective and lessen self-criticism.
- **Work with a Therapist:** Therapy can help you address negative self-talk in a structured way, equipping you with tools to replace critical thoughts with constructive ones.

9. Visualize a Positive Future

- **Create a Vision Board:** Visualize a future that excites you, whether it includes new goals, hobbies, relationships, or simply feeling at peace.
- **Set Personal Goals:** Focus on new personal or professional goals. Working toward something positive can distract from negativity and give you a sense of purpose and excitement.

10. Celebrate Your Strength and Resilience

- **Recognize Progress:** Acknowledge how far you've come, even if the steps feel small. Each step forward is proof of your strength and resilience.
- **Honor Your Courage:** Divorce takes courage, and getting through it is an accomplishment in itself. Celebrate the fact that you're taking steps toward a healthier future.

Replacing negative self-talk with supportive, compassionate thoughts takes time, but these strategies can help you retrain your mind to focus on growth, strength, and positivity as you navigate through this challenging period.

ENGAGING IN ACTIVITIES

THAT BOOST CONFIDENCE

Engaging in activities that boost confidence during a divorce can help you rediscover your sense of self, build resilience, and foster a positive outlook for the future. Here's how you can start:

1. Pursue New Hobbies and Interests

Try an activity you've always wanted to do, like painting, dancing, or learning a musical instrument. Exploring new interests can renew your sense of self and boost confidence. Engage in activities you once enjoyed but set aside. Revisiting familiar interests can remind you of your strengths and talents.

2. Focus on Physical Fitness

Physical activity releases endorphins, which improve mood and reduce stress. A consistent routine can also make you feel stronger and more accomplished. Try a confidence-boosting class like kickboxing, yoga, or dance. These activities promote confidence and self-discipline to help you feel physically and mentally empowered.

3. Set Personal and Professional Goals

Visualizing what you want to achieve can give you

motivation and a sense of purpose, helping you move forward with confidence. Start small and build momentum. As you reach each goal, you'll feel a sense of accomplishment that reinforces self-worth.

4. Invest in Self-Care and Personal Style

Dressing in a way that makes you feel good can significantly boost your confidence. Choose clothing that feels authentic to you and makes you feel empowered. Try a new hairstyle, skincare routine, or a self-care day to help you feel refreshed and renewed. When you feel good physically, it often translates to feeling good emotionally.

5. Practice Positive Self-Talk and Affirmations

Use affirmations daily and repeat affirmations like "I am capable," "I am resilient," or "I am building a beautiful future." Regularly reinforcing positive thoughts can increase confidence over time. Replace negative thoughts with positives when doubts arise, and counter them with supportive, encouraging thoughts. For instance, replace "I'm not good enough" with "I am growing and learning each day."

6. Strengthen Your Social Network

Spend time with people who uplift and encourage

you. Supportive relationships can reaffirm your worth and remind you that you're not alone. Whether it's a class, a hobby group, or a support group, connecting with others in positive environments can provide comfort, build confidence, and even lead to new friendships.

7. Take Classes to Develop New Skills

Focus on personal development by signing up for workshops or online courses that interest you, like cooking, photography, or public speaking. Learning new skills can give you a sense of achievement. If work-related, skill-building can enhance your job performance and confidence in your professional abilities, helping you feel empowered and self-sufficient.

8. Volunteer or Give Back

Volunteering can remind you of your strengths and positively impact those in need. Helping others often brings a renewed sense of purpose and fulfillment. Sharing your knowledge and supporting others can affirm your self-worth and allow you to see the positive impact you're capable of making.

9. Challenge Yourself Gradually

Step out of your comfort zone and take small, manageable risks, like trying a new activity solo or speaking in front of a group. Each challenge you face successfully builds confidence. Acknowledge each achievement, no matter how small. Building confidence is a gradual process, and celebrating steps forward can encourage more growth.

10. Reflect on Strengths and Achievements

Write down moments when you felt strong, accomplished, or proud. Reflecting on these successes reinforces self-confidence and reminds you of your capabilities. List things you appreciate about yourself and your life, like personal qualities or past accomplishments. Focusing on the positives helps build a more confident outlook.

By regularly engaging in activities that uplift and challenge you, you can rebuild your confidence, discover new passions, and develop a stronger sense of independence and self-worth during and after your divorce.

SETTING PERSONAL GOALS

Setting personal goals during a divorce can help you stay focused, feel empowered, and create a roadmap for a brighter future. Here are some effective steps to guide you in setting meaningful and achievable goals during this time:

1. Reflect on Your Needs and Values

Take time to consider what matters to you, such as financial independence, emotional healing, personal growth, or strengthening relationships. Think about the person you want to become after the divorce. Let this vision guide the types of goals you set, whether they're related to health, career, or personal well-being.

2. Set Short-Term and Long-Term Goals

Break down your long-term goals. For big goals, like financial security or career growth, set smaller, short-term goals that are achievable within days or weeks. These create a sense of progress and keep you motivated.

Balance immediate needs and future ambitions by setting short-term goals for things that bring immediate stability (like budgeting or finding a new place to live) alongside long-term goals that give you hope and excitement for the future.

3. Focus on Different Life Areas

Set goals that focus on self-improvement, such as reading more, practicing mindfulness, or journaling regularly. Include physical goals like exercising a few times a week, adopting healthier eating habits, or getting more sleep. Establish financial goals, such as creating a budget, setting up a savings plan, or consulting a financial advisor if needed. Set goals for nurturing existing relationships, meeting new people, or joining supportive communities.

4. Use the SMART Goal Framework

- **Specific:** Make each goal clear and specific. For example, instead of "get in shape," try "walk for 30 minutes three times a week."
- **Measurable:** Add ways to measure progress. A goal like "save $500 per month" is measurable and helps you stay on track.
- **Achievable:** Be realistic about what you can accomplish based on your current resources and circumstances.
- **Relevant:** Ensure the goal aligns with your needs and values. Ask if it contributes to your well-being and future vision.

- **Time-Bound:** Set a timeline, even if it's flexible. Having a timeframe adds structure to your goals, like aiming to save a certain amount by the end of the month.

5. Prioritize Self-Care Goals

- **Emotional Healing:** Set specific goals around emotional well-being, like "attend therapy once a week" or "journal for 10 minutes each day."
- **Routine Self-Care:** Incorporate relaxing or fulfilling activities, such as taking up a hobby, practicing yoga, or dedicating time to meditation.

6. Embrace Growth and Learning Goals

Set a goal to learn something new, whether it's a cooking class, a foreign language, or a professional skill. Learning fosters confidence and opens new possibilities. Use this time to understand yourself better. Set goals like "write in a gratitude journal every day" or "list five strengths I want to cultivate."

7. Set Boundaries and Relationship Goals

Set goals that help you manage interactions with your ex-spouse if needed, such as "set clear boundaries for communication" or "keep conversations brief and focused on co-parenting." Aim to connect with positive, supportive people. This could be as simple as "reach out to one friend each week" or "join a local support group."

8. Celebrate Progress and Small Wins

Acknowledge each step you achieve. Small rewards can motivate you to stay committed and show you how far you're coming. Keep a journal or checklist of your progress, noting what you've accomplished. Seeing these milestones can be encouraging and give you the confidence to keep going.

9. Reevaluate and Adjust Goals as Needed

Life circumstances may change as you progress through your divorce, so adjust your goals to reflect your current needs and resources. As you start achieving initial goals, you may find new priorities emerging. Don't hesitate to redefine your focus to stay aligned with what feels meaningful.

10. Visualize Success and Stay Positive

Visualization can be a powerful tool for motivation. Take time each day to picture yourself achieving your goals and living the life you desire. Setbacks may occur, but remind yourself that each step forward is progress. Focus on how these goals are helping you build a fulfilling, independent life.

Setting and working toward personal goals gives you a sense of purpose, stability, and empowerment during this transitional period. These goals are tools to help you find clarity, resilience, and growth as you shape the next chapter of your life.

Chapter 8: Redefining Your Identity

DISCOVERING WHO YOU ARE OUTSIDE OF MARRIAGE

Discovering who you are outside of marriage after a divorce can feel both exciting and challenging, as it's an opportunity to rediscover your identity, values, and passions. Here are some steps to guide you in reconnecting with yourself and building a fulfilling, independent life:

1. Reflect on Your Values and Beliefs

Take time to examine what truly matters to you now. Write down your values, such as independence, growth, kindness, or creativity. This helps you ground your identity in what's most meaningful to you. Reflect on how your beliefs about life, relationships, and success may have changed. Embrace any shifts in perspective as part of your evolving self.

2. Reconnect with Past Hobbies and Passions

Reflect on pre-marriage interests. Think about activities or hobbies you loved before marriage but may have set aside. Reconnecting with these can reignite old passions and remind you of your unique interests. Experiment with new activities that interest you. Whether it's painting, hiking, writing, or dancing, trying new things can help you discover sides of yourself you didn't know existed.

3. Define Personal Goals and Dreams

Use this time to think about what you want to accomplish on your own. Whether it's traveling, advancing in your career, or simply finding peace, having personal goals gives you a sense of purpose. Visualize the life you want by putting together a vision board with images, quotes, and symbols of your future goals. This can give you direction and inspiration as you rediscover yourself.

4. Explore Your Strengths and Weaknesses

Recognize your strengths and reflect on your qualities, achievements, and the strengths that helped you through tough times. Embrace these as part of your identity. Identify any areas you'd like to develop, like confidence, assertiveness, or emotional resilience. Embracing both strengths and growth areas helps you gain self-awareness and confidence.

5. Cultivate Independence

Develop daily and weekly routines that are just for you, like an evening walk, a morning coffee ritual, or a creative session. Routines can help you feel grounded and reinforce your independence. Empower yourself by learning skills that can improve your life, such as managing finances, cooking, or taking up a craft. This builds confidence and reinforces your self-reliance.

6. Spend Quality Time Alone

- **Enjoy Solitude:** Spend time doing things alone to get comfortable with your own company. Solo activities like reading, walking, or having a "date" with yourself can help you reconnect with who you are outside of a relationship.
- **Practice Mindfulness or Meditation:** These practices help you tune in to your thoughts, feelings, and needs, fostering a deeper understanding of yourself without outside influences.

7. Reconnect with Friends and Build New Relationships

Spend time with friends who support you and appreciate you for who you are. This can give you confidence and a sense of belonging. Joining social groups, clubs, or classes can introduce you to new friends who share your interests. New connections can give you fresh perspectives and opportunities for growth.

8. Focus on Emotional Healing and Personal Growth

- **Seek Therapy or Counseling:** Therapy can be a powerful way to explore your feelings, work through pain, and understand yourself better.
- **Read Personal Development Books:** Books on self-discovery, personal growth, and self-care can provide inspiration and guidance on your journey of rediscovery.

9. Challenge Yourself with New Experiences

Try something new and bold, whether it's traveling alone, starting a new job, or taking a class that challenges you. Pushing your limits helps you grow and discover what you're capable of. Acknowledge each step you take toward discovering yourself.

Recognizing your progress, no matter how small, reinforces your sense of self and builds confidence.

10. Be Patient and Kind with Yourself

- **Allow Time for Self-Discovery:** Remember that rediscovering yourself is a process that can take time. Allow yourself to grow and change at your own pace.
- **Celebrate Your Resilience:** Divorce can be painful, but it also shows your strength. Embrace this strength as part of your identity and take pride in how far you've come.

Rediscovering yourself after a divorce is a journey of growth and self-love. Embracing new experiences, personal goals, and time alone can help you reconnect with who you are and build a fulfilling life beyond marriage.

PURSUING HOBBIES AND INTERESTS

Pursuing hobbies and interests after a divorce is a great way to rediscover yourself, find joy, and create a new chapter in life. Here's how to get started:

1. Reconnect with Past Interests

Think about what you loved doing before marriage. Revisit activities like painting, reading, or playing a musical instrument that may have brought you joy. Start small by dedicating a few hours each week. Revisiting familiar interests helps you feel connected to yourself and can be comforting during a transitional time.

2. Try New Hobbies and Explore Fresh Interests

Make a "Bucket List" of activities and list things you've always wanted to try, like pottery, rock climbing, or cooking classes. Exploring new hobbies opens you up to possibilities you may not have considered. Try a few different activities to see what resonates. Many community centers or online platforms offer trial classes, so you can dip your toes into multiple interests.

3. Engage in Physical Activities

Getting active with Physical hobbies like yoga, dancing, hiking, or biking is excellent for both physical and mental health. Exercise releases endorphins that can improve mood and reduce stress. Group fitness or dance classes can add social interaction to your routine, helping you meet new people while doing something you enjoy.

4. Take Up Creative Outlets

Creative pursuits like painting, journaling, photography, or learning an instrument can be therapeutic and help you process emotions. Work on something you can immerse yourself in, like writing a story, knitting, or starting a home garden. Creating something can be deeply fulfilling and rewarding.

5. Explore Hobbies for Self-Improvement

Look for skill-building hobbies, like cooking, coding, or public speaking. Developing skills can build confidence and open new doors in your personal or professional life. Many platforms offer free or affordable classes, allowing you to learn anything from photography to language skills, giving you a sense of accomplishment and growth.

6. Join Social Clubs or Interest Groups

Check out meetups or clubs for book lovers, runners, or even trivia enthusiasts. These groups offer a sense of community and camaraderie around shared interests. Being around others with similar interests can be energizing and help you form new friendships, which can be especially beneficial after a divorce.

7. Schedule "You" Time Regularly

Create a routine by setting aside dedicated time for hobbies. Whether it's every Saturday morning or a couple of evenings a week, this routine gives you something to look forward to. Make your hobbies part of your lifestyle, even if only for 15–30 minutes a day. Consistency brings fulfillment and helps the activity become a natural part of your life.

8. Use Hobbies for Self-Care and Relaxation

Practice mindful hobbies like meditation, gardening, or journaling to help you relax and focus on yourself. Hobbies don't have to be grand. Simple activities like trying new recipes or stargazing can bring joy and comfort.

9. Challenge Yourself with Goal-Oriented Hobbies

- **Set Personal Challenges:** If you're into fitness, aim for a race; if you love reading, set a goal to read a certain number of books. Goals provide motivation and a sense of accomplishment.
- **Track Your Progress:** Documenting your progress through photos, journals, or achievements keeps you motivated and lets you see how far you've

come.

10. Embrace the Joy of Discovery

Keep an open mind as some activities may surprise you. Be open to trying things outside your comfort zone, even if they feel unfamiliar. Focus on enjoyment, not perfection as you enjoy the journey of learning and exploring, rather than focusing on mastering every activity. This mindset allows you to relax and appreciate each experience.

Pursuing hobbies after a divorce helps you reconnect with yourself, discover new passions, and build a fulfilling, balanced life. These interests can become a source of joy, comfort, and self-expression as you move forward into a new chapter.

EMBRACING INDEPENDENCE

Embracing independence during a divorce is both empowering and essential for moving forward confidently. It's about redefining who you are, gaining self-reliance, and building a fulfilling life on your terms. Here's how to embrace independence throughout this journey:

1. Acknowledge Your Strength and Resilience

Acknowledge the courage it takes to go through a divorce and remind yourself that you're capable of handling challenges. Give yourself credit for each step, no matter how small. Completing paperwork, setting up your own space, or handling new responsibilities are all wins worth celebrating.

2. Take Ownership of Your Decisions

Divorce can lead to self-doubt, but remember that you're the best person to make decisions for your life. Trust in your ability to make choices that serve your happiness and well-being. Be clear about your needs and boundaries, whether with your ex, friends, or family. Assertiveness reinforces self-respect and independence.

3. Set Personal Goals for Your New Chapter

Define your vision and picture the kind of life you want as a single person. Do you see yourself advancing in your career, traveling more, or taking up new hobbies? Use this vision to set meaningful goals. Break large goals into small, achievable steps. Taking action towards goals builds momentum and a sense of purpose, reinforcing your independence.

4. Create a New Routine and Space

Building routines around self-care, work, and hobbies give structure to your day and a feeling of stability. If you're in a new home or adjusting your current space, make it yours. Add items, colors, and touches that reflect your personality. Creating a space you love fosters a sense of autonomy and belonging.

5. Develop Financial Independence

Take time to understand your income, expenses, and financial goals. Budgeting and setting up savings give you control and peace of mind. If needed, consult a financial advisor. They can help you make informed decisions, such as investing or managing assets, to support your financial independence.

6. Build a Supportive Network

Surround yourself with supportive friends and family who encourage your independence and growth. Join groups, clubs, or online communities where you can meet people with shared interests. These new connections can add positive influences to your life.

7. Discover and Pursue Your Passions

Explore hobbies or passions you may have set

aside during your marriage. Rediscovering these can be deeply rewarding. Challenge yourself with new experiences, whether learning a skill, taking a class, or joining a club. Exploring your interests on your terms reinforces self-identity and independence.

8. Develop Problem-Solving Skills

Face challenges head-on as divorce often brings new responsibilities, from managing finances to maintaining a home. Embrace these as opportunities to develop practical skills. Don't be afraid to ask for help or research new skills. Building self-sufficiency can increase your confidence and sense of control.

9. Focus on Self-Compassion and Self-Care

Divorce can be emotionally draining, so prioritize self-compassion. Remind yourself that this is a period of adjustment, and it's okay to move at your own pace. Engage in activities that nurture your body, mind, and spirit, like exercise, meditation, journaling, or pampering routines.

10. Embrace the Freedom to Rediscover Yourself

Take time to think about who you are now and what you want from life. Journaling, therapy, or meditation can help you connect with your inner self. Use this time to explore what independence means to you. With freedom comes the opportunity to redefine your life and choose a path that reflects your new life.

Chapter 9: Co-Parenting Challenges and Solutions

EFFECTIVE COMMUNICATION WITH YOUR EX-SPOUSE

Effective communication with an ex-spouse while co-parenting is essential, especially during the challenging transition of divorce. Here are some strategies to help ensure smoother interactions:

1. **Stay Child-Focused:** Make your child's well-being the priority in every conversation. If a discussion starts to shift toward personal grievances or past issues, gently redirect it back to parenting topics.
2. **Establish Clear Boundaries:** Decide on what topics are appropriate to discuss and stick

to those. Avoid revisiting past conflicts or personal issues unrelated to your child.
3. **Use Neutral and Respectful Language:** Keep your tone calm and professional. This can help prevent defensive reactions and keep the focus on parenting.
4. **Create a Co-Parenting Communication Plan:** Agree on a structured way to communicate—whether it's through email, a shared calendar, or a parenting app like OurFamilyWizard. Structured communication reduces misunderstandings and keeps conversations organized.
5. **Be Concise and Specific:** When making requests or suggestions, be clear and direct. Avoid long messages that could open the door to misinterpretation or argument.
6. **Be Open to Compromise:** Approach each discussion with flexibility. Recognize that compromise may be necessary to maintain a healthy co-parenting relationship.
7. **Choose the Right Time:** Don't bring up important matters at stressful or inconvenient times. Try to schedule conversations or ask if it's a good time to talk. This approach respects each other's schedules and ensures both are prepared for a productive discussion.
8. **Listen Actively:** Show your ex-spouse that you're genuinely considering their perspective. Active listening can foster

mutual respect and encourage a cooperative relationship.
9. **Keep Emotions in Check:** If emotions are running high, it's okay to take a break and revisit the topic later. Calm communication helps prevent escalation.
10. **Put Agreements in Writing:** To avoid confusion, consider putting any parenting agreements, schedules, or decisions in writing. This can provide a reference point if disagreements arise.

Using these methods can help maintain a cooperative, productive co-parenting relationship that prioritizes your child's needs, even during personal challenges.

HANDLING CONFLICTS AND DISAGREEMENTS

Handling conflicts and disagreements while co-parenting during a divorce requires clear communication, mutual respect, and a focus on the well-being of your children. Here's a guide to navigating these challenges in a way that promotes positive outcomes for everyone involved:

1. Prioritize the Children's Well-Being

- **Keep Kids at the Center, Not in the Middle:** Make decisions and communicate in ways that protect your children from conflict. Focus on what's best for them, rather than personal grievances.
- **Consider Their Emotional Needs:** Kids are sensitive to the tension between parents, so prioritize their stability and happiness by maintaining a peaceful co-parenting relationship.

2. Establish Clear Boundaries and Agreements

- **Create a Co-Parenting Plan:** Work with your ex-spouse to outline clear guidelines for custody, visitation, communication, and decision-making. A well-defined plan reduces ambiguity and potential conflicts.
- **Agree on Boundaries:** Discuss boundaries related to communication frequency, parenting decisions, and involvement with each other's personal lives. Boundaries provide structure and prevent unnecessary misunderstandings.

3. Communicate Respectfully and Directly

- **Use Neutral Language:** Avoid blame or accusations. Stick to "I" statements and focus on specific issues rather than personal attacks (e.g., "I'm concerned about the bedtime routine" instead of "You always let them stay up late").
- **Listen Actively:** Practice active listening, giving your co-parent the chance to express their views. Even if you disagree, understanding their perspective can lead to more effective solutions.

4. Use a Child-Focused Communication Platform

- **Consider a Co-Parenting App:** Many apps are designed for co-parenting, allowing parents to coordinate schedules, share information, and communicate. Using a platform focused on co-parenting can reduce misunderstandings.
- **Keep Communication Business-Like:** Treat your interactions as professional exchanges. Avoid emotional language and keep conversations focused on logistics and the needs of your children.

5. Stay Flexible and Open to Compromise

- **Be Open to Adjustments:** Children's needs change over time, so it's essential to stay flexible with

schedules and agreements. Small compromises show cooperation and can reduce conflict.
- **Focus on Give and Take:** Remember that both parents are adjusting, so try to support each other when possible. If you're flexible on a specific issue, your co-parent may be more willing to reciprocate in the future.

6. Manage Your Own Emotions

- **Pause Before Responding:** When emotions run high, take a moment to breathe or step away before responding. Approaching conflicts with a calm mindset prevents escalation.
- **Seek Support:** If the situation triggers strong emotions, consider speaking with a therapist or trusted friend rather than venting to your co-parent. Processing emotions independently helps you stay objective in co-parenting conversations.

7. Avoid Involving Children in Conflicts

- **Keep Disagreements Private:** Never argue or discuss disagreements in front of the children. This helps them feel secure and minimizes stress.
- **Respect the Other Parent in Front of the Kids:** Speak positively or neutrally about your co-

parent when your children are around. This models respect and reassure them that they don't have to "choose sides."

8. Seek Mediation if Needed

- **Consider Professional Mediation:** If conflicts persist, a neutral mediator can help you work through difficult issues. Mediation can lead to more effective, structured solutions that benefit the children.
- **Find Supportive Resources:** Some communities offer co-parenting classes or support groups that provide strategies for managing disagreements. Learning with other parents facing similar challenges can be reassuring and helpful.

9. Focus on Shared Goals and Values

- **Identify Common Ground:** Reflect on shared goals for your children's future, like education, health, and happiness. Focusing on these common values can help both parents set aside differences.
- **Respect Differences in Parenting Styles:** Accept that your ex-spouse's approach to parenting may differ from yours. As long as it's not harmful to the children, allow them the freedom to parent in

their own way.

10. Reassess and Adjust as Needed

- **Review Agreements Periodically:** Co-parenting plans may need adjustment over time. Regularly reviewing and updating the plan ensures that it continues to meet everyone's needs.
- **Stay Open to Improvement:** Learn from past conflicts and make changes to avoid similar issues in the future. Continuous improvement helps both parents grow and build a healthier co-parenting relationship.

By handling conflicts with patience, respect, and a focus on the children's needs, you can create a more peaceful co-parenting relationship. Though disagreements are natural, managing them constructively will help create a stable environment for your children and a cooperative dynamic for both parents.

ENSURING A STABLE ENVIRONMENT FOR YOUR CHILDREN

Creating a stable environment for your children while co-parenting during a divorce helps them feel secure and loved, even amid major changes. Here are ways to foster consistency, stability, and emotional support for your kids:

1. Maintain Consistent Routines

Work with your co-parent to create a consistent routine for school, meals, bedtime, and activities across both households. A stable schedule provides kids with a sense of normalcy. Follow the agreed-upon schedule for custody and visitation as closely as possible. Consistency helps children feel more secure in their relationships with both parents.

2. Create a Safe, Comfortable Space in Each Home

Provide children with a dedicated space in each home, such as their room or a personalized corner. Familiar items, like blankets, toys, or photos, help them feel at home. Keep similar bedtime rituals or morning routines in both households. Familiarity helps children feel comfortable no matter where they are.

3. Communicate Clearly and Calmly

Let children know about schedules, upcoming transitions, or any changes in routine in advance. This helps them feel prepared and reduces anxiety.

Keep communication with your co-parent civil, especially around the children. When they see you communicate respectfully, it reassures them that both parents are committed to their well-being.

4. Show Unified Parenting

Work with your co-parent to establish consistent rules, such as homework expectations, screen time limits, and behavior standards. A united front shows children that both parents are aligned on important values. While maintaining core rules, understand that your co-parent may have slightly different parenting styles. As long as it doesn't negatively impact the kids, flexibility on minor differences can reduce conflict.

5. Provide Emotional Support and Reassurance

Let children know they can talk to you about their feelings. Validating their emotions reassures them that it's okay to feel sad, angry, or confused. Regularly remind your children that the divorce is not their fault and that both parents love them unconditionally. This assurance is crucial for their sense of security.

6. Avoid Negative Talk About the Other Parent

Avoid arguing or discussing conflicts with your co-parent in front of the children. Shielding them from adult issues allows them to have a positive view of both parents. When talking about your co-parent, use neutral or positive language. This helps children feel comfortable in their relationship with both parents.

7. Maintain Regular Contact with Both Parents

Encourage your children's relationship with the other parent, even when they're not in their physical custody. Phone calls, video chats, and text messages provide emotional continuity. Allow children to connect with their other parents freely and without guilt. A strong bond with both parents is essential for their emotional health.

8. Keep Changes to a Minimum

Try to keep other aspects of life (such as school, extracurriculars, and friendships) as steady as possible. Minimizing changes in their environment helps kids adjust more easily to the family transition. When moving from one home to another, ensure the transition is calm and predictable. A simple "welcome back" routine or favorite snack can make transitions less stressful.

9. Support Their Social and Academic Life

Both parents should aim to stay engaged in school events, activities, and milestones. Showing up for important moments reinforces stability in their lives. Allow kids to maintain their friendships and participate in activities they enjoy. These relationships give them an additional source of support and normalcy.

10. Seek Outside Help if Needed

A child therapist can help kids process their emotions and navigate the changes of divorce. Counseling can be an excellent tool for building resilience and stability. Let children know they can also talk to other trusted adults, like family members or teachers if they need extra support.

11. Model Positivity and Resilience

Show your children that even though things may be difficult, you're handling them with resilience. Positive role modeling teaches them that challenges can be managed. Highlight the benefits of having two loving homes or the special time they get with each parent. Focusing on the positive can help children feel optimistic about the future.

By following these strategies, you can create a nurturing, stable environment for your children as you co-parent through divorce. This stability helps them feel supported, loved, and secure during a time of change.

Chapter 10: Legal Finalization and Moving Forward

UNDERSTANDING THE FINAL STEPS OF THE DIVORCE PROCESS

The final steps of the divorce process can feel both overwhelming and relieving. Here's a breakdown to help you understand what to expect and how to navigate these last steps:

1. Review the Final Divorce Agreement

- **Property and Asset Division:** Ensure you understand how all assets and debts will be divided, including bank accounts, retirement plans, investments, real estate, and personal property.

- **Child Custody and Support Arrangements:** If applicable, confirm custody schedules, support payments, and any shared responsibilities for your children.
- **Spousal Support (Alimony):** Be sure you understand the amount, frequency, and duration of any spousal support obligations or entitlements.
- **Miscellaneous Agreements:** Review agreements on other terms, such as who will handle shared pets or any specific financial accounts.

2. Sign the Settlement Agreement

Once you and your spouse agree on all terms, you'll sign a settlement or separation agreement. This document legally binds both parties to the terms outlined.

If you're working with attorneys, they will often review this agreement with you to ensure it's accurate and complete.

3. File the Agreement with the Court

Your attorney or you (if you're representing yourself) will submit the signed agreement to the court for approval. Some jurisdictions require a final hearing to approve the agreement, while others only require paperwork.

The judge will review to confirm that the terms are fair and meet any legal requirements, especially concerning child custody and support if children are involved.

4. Attend the Final Divorce Hearing (if required)

Some courts mandate a final hearing where a judge will ask brief questions to confirm both parties agree to the divorce terms. In uncontested divorces, this may be a straightforward hearing where the judge officially finalizes the divorce.

5. Receive the Divorce Decree

Once the judge approves, you'll receive a divorce decree or judgment of divorce. This legal document finalizes the divorce and outlines the agreed-upon terms, making them enforceable by law. Keep a certified copy of this decree in a safe place, as you may need it to update personal records or for financial or legal purposes.

6. Update Legal and Financial Documents

After the divorce is finalized, update your legal

documents (such as wills, powers of attorney, and beneficiaries on insurance policies) and financial records (like bank accounts and credit cards). Notify relevant institutions, such as your bank, employer, and government offices, to reflect your new status or name if it has changed.

7. Follow Up on Settlement Terms

If the agreement requires ongoing steps—like spousal support payments or asset transfers—ensure you understand your responsibilities and timelines. Stay organized with a calendar or reminders to keep track of important deadlines related to your settlement.

Understanding these final steps can help you feel more prepared as you move through the process. With everything in place, you can focus on transitioning to your new chapter and begin building a life that reflects your goals and needs.

ENSURING ALL LEGAL MATTERS ARE SETTLED

Ensuring all legal matters are settled during a divorce is essential for a smooth transition and to avoid issues in the future. Here's a guide on how to cover all your legal bases:

1. Get a Clear Understanding of Divorce Laws in Your State

Divorce laws vary by state, affecting how property, debts, child custody, and support are handled. Consult with an attorney or research to ensure you're informed about specific laws that apply to your situation.

2. Organize and Disclose Financial Documents

Collect all financial records, including bank statements, investment accounts, tax returns, pay stubs, retirement accounts, mortgage documents, credit card statements, and debts. Ensure complete transparency; withholding information or assets can lead to legal penalties and may void agreements.

3. Ensure Full Division of Assets and Debts

Work with your attorney to create a thorough inventory of marital assets and debts. Understand how property is divided in your state—whether by equitable distribution or community property laws—and ensure the agreement reflects this.

Don't forget smaller assets like furniture, electronics, or personal items, as well as debts such as joint loans or credit cards.

4. Address Spousal Support (Alimony)

If one spouse is entitled to support, agree on the type, duration, and amount. Spousal support can be temporary or permanent, depending on state laws and the specific financial situation. Document the terms in the divorce agreement to make it enforceable.

5. Settle Child Custody and Support Matters

If you have children, work out a custody arrangement that prioritizes their well-being and stability. This includes physical custody (where the children live) and legal custody (who makes major decisions).

Arrange for child support based on state guidelines, which usually consider income and custody arrangements.

Include provisions for parenting schedules, holidays, and decision-making responsibilities to minimize future conflicts.

6. Revise Your Estate Plan and Beneficiaries

Update your will, powers of attorney, and any health directives, as well as beneficiaries on life insurance policies, retirement accounts, and investment accounts. Without changes, your ex-spouse may still be entitled to benefits in case of your passing.

7. Address Future Tax Implications

Understand how alimony, child support, and asset division impact taxes. For instance, alimony is generally no longer tax-deductible or taxable for divorces finalized after 2018, but other factors may still influence tax responsibilities. Work with a tax advisor if possible, to understand filing status changes, claiming dependents, and capital gains tax on transferred assets.

8. Consider a Qualified Domestic Relations Order (QDRO) for Retirement Accounts

If dividing retirement accounts, a QDRO may be required to ensure that funds are distributed without penalty. This is a court order that allows for the division of qualified retirement plans like 401(k)s and pensions.

9. Obtain a Written Agreement for All Settlements

All agreements—whether for custody, support, asset division, or any other aspect—should be written into a formal settlement agreement. This document will be submitted to the court and incorporated into the final divorce decree, making it legally binding and enforceable.

10. Stay Committed to Open and Timely Communication with Your Attorney

Regularly update your attorney on any changes or new issues that arise. This helps ensure your legal strategy covers all developments, especially if the divorce process extends over time.

11. Finalize All Settlement Terms Before the Divorce Decree

Make sure all terms are settled and documented in your final divorce decree or judgment. After the divorce is finalized, it can be difficult to change the terms without going through a separate legal process.

12. Confirm Compliance with Court Orders and Follow Up on Implementation

After the divorce is complete, follow up on any actions you're required to take, such as transferring property titles, updating beneficiaries, or paying support. Track these requirements and ensure everything is done according to the court's orders to prevent legal issues later on.

By addressing these areas, you'll have greater peace of mind knowing your legal matters are handled comprehensively, setting you up for a more stable future post-divorce.

PLANNING FOR YOUR FUTURE POST-DIVORCE

Planning for your future post-divorce during the divorce process can be empowering and help you transition into a new chapter with confidence. Taking practical steps toward your personal, financial, and emotional goals will set a strong foundation. Here's how to approach it:

1. Clarify Your Goals and Vision for the Future

- **Visualize Your Ideal Life:** Take time to imagine what you want your life to look like post-divorce.

Think about your career, living arrangements, relationships, and personal interests. This vision will guide your decisions and help you focus on what truly matters.

- **Set Short- and Long-Term Goals:** Identify both immediate goals (such as setting up a new household or rebuilding your social circle) and long-term ones (like advancing your career or saving for retirement). Specific goals create a roadmap for the future.

2. Establish Financial Independence

- **Evaluate Your Finances:** Assess your income, expenses, assets, and debts. Understanding your financial situation allows you to make informed choices about budgeting and saving.
- **Create a Post-Divorce Budget:** Develop a realistic budget based on your current income and expenses, accounting for any changes that may come after the divorce. Adjusting to a single income will give you financial stability and peace of mind.
- **Build an Emergency Fund:** Setting aside savings for unexpected expenses is essential to secure your future. Aim for three to six months' worth of living expenses in an emergency fund to provide

a safety net.

3. Understand Your Legal and Financial Rights

- **Consult Financial and Legal Experts:** During the divorce, work with a financial advisor or attorney to understand your rights regarding alimony, child support, division of assets, and retirement benefits. Protecting your financial future is essential.
- **Review Insurance and Benefits:** Make sure you have adequate health, life, and home insurance for yourself and your dependents. Update your beneficiaries and consider any new coverage you may need.

4. Build a New Support Network

- **Strengthen Relationships with Friends and Family:** Lean on trusted friends and family members for emotional support and encouragement. A reliable support network helps you stay motivated and focused on the future.
- **Join Support Groups or Communities:** Connect with others who have been through a divorce, either in person or online. These connections can provide empathy, advice, and new friendships as you rebuild your social network.

5. Focus on Personal Growth and Development

- **Invest in Your Education or Career:** Consider furthering your education, learning a new skill, or taking on a new job role. Professional development can open doors and boost your financial independence.
- **Rediscover Your Interests:** Engage in hobbies or passions you may have set aside. Pursuing activities you enjoy helps you reconnect with yourself and fills your life with positive experiences.

6. Create a Self-Care Routine

- **Prioritize Physical and Mental Health:** Take care of your health through exercise, nutritious meals, and sufficient sleep. Staying active and healthy keeps your energy levels high and improves resilience.
- **Develop Emotional Resilience:** Practice mindfulness, journal, or work with a therapist to process your feelings and find emotional stability. These habits help you manage stress and build a strong foundation for the future.

7. Consider Future Living Arrangements

- **Decide on Housing Needs:** Think about whether you want to stay in your current home or relocate. Consider what type of environment would best support your emotional and financial well-being.
- **Plan for Your Family's Needs:** If you have children, involve them in discussions about potential moves. A stable home environment is crucial for their sense of security and helps them feel settled.

8. Revisit Estate Planning

- **Update Your Will and Beneficiaries:** After the divorce, review your will, trusts, and any beneficiaries on insurance policies, retirement accounts, or other financial assets.
- **Consider Future Inheritance and Custody Arrangements:** If you have dependents, plan for guardianship and ensure they're financially protected. Consulting an estate planner can help ensure your assets are managed according to your wishes.

9. Cultivate a Positive Mindset for the Future

- **Practice Gratitude:** Focus on the positive aspects

of your life, both current and future. Reflecting on what you're grateful for can improve your outlook and motivate you to pursue your goals.
- **Embrace Change:** Remind yourself that change can lead to growth and new opportunities. Viewing your future as a fresh start allows you to move forward with optimism and confidence.

10. Track Your Progress and Adjust as Needed

- **Review and Reflect:** Regularly revisit your goals and check in with yourself to see how far you've come. Adjust your plans as your needs and desires evolve.
- **Celebrate Small Wins:** Recognize the progress you're making, even in small ways. Acknowledging your efforts and successes builds confidence and keeps you motivated.

By planning carefully, focusing on your growth, and prioritizing your well-being, you can set yourself up for a rewarding and independent life post-divorce. Taking these steps during the divorce process not only prepares you for a stable future but also helps you feel empowered and optimistic about what lies ahead.

Chapter 11: Long-Term Financial Planning

INVESTING AND SAVING FOR THE FUTURE

Going through a divorce often reshapes your financial landscape, so taking proactive steps to invest and save for long-term financial security is essential. Here's a roadmap to help you build a solid financial foundation during and after divorce:

1. Establish a Post-Divorce Budget

Start with a realistic budget that accounts for your new income and expenses. Include child or spousal support payments if applicable. Track your spending and adjust as needed to ensure you're living within your means. A clear budget gives you a baseline to allocate funds for savings and investments.

2. Build an Emergency Fund

Prioritize building an emergency fund with 3-6 months' worth of living expenses. This safety net helps protect you from financial strain in case of unexpected expenses or income fluctuations. If saving a large amount seems daunting, start small—aim for one month of expenses, then gradually add to it.

3. Reevaluate Your Investment Goals

Think about your financial goals, including retirement, buying a home, or supporting your children's education. Understanding these goals will guide your investment strategy. Consider working with a financial advisor, especially if you're uncertain about where to begin. They can help set realistic, attainable goals and guide you on the best investment vehicles.

4. Diversify Your Investments

Diversifying is crucial to reduce risk and build long-term wealth. Consider a mix of stocks, bonds, mutual funds, or real estate based on your risk tolerance and time horizon. For lower-risk, long-term investments, consider index funds or exchange-traded funds (ETFs), which provide diversified exposure to the market and generally have lower fees.

5. Maximize Retirement Contributions

Contribute to retirement accounts like a 401(k) or IRA. If you're employed, contribute enough to get any employer match if offered—it's essentially "free" money. For higher retirement savings, consider maxing out contributions to your 401(k) or IRA. Remember, the earlier you start, the more time your money has to grow with compound interest.

6. Plan for Health Savings with an HSA

If you have a high-deductible health plan (HDHP), consider contributing to a Health Savings Account (HSA). HSAs provide tax advantages, and funds roll over from year to year. HSA funds can be used for qualified medical expenses and, after age 65, can even be withdrawn for non-medical expenses, similar to a retirement account.

7. Consider 529 Plans for Children's Education

If you have children and plan to contribute to their education, a 529 college savings plan offers tax advantages for education-related expenses. Contributions grow tax-free, and withdrawals for qualified education expenses are also tax-free, helping you save for your child's future.

8. Adjust Your Insurance Coverage

Review and update your insurance policies, including health, life, and disability insurance, to reflect your new situation. Ensure you have adequate coverage, especially if you're the primary custodian of children or have financial dependents. Life insurance can provide a financial safety net for them in case of an emergency.

9. Be Cautious with Large Purchases and Debt

Try to avoid taking on new debt or making major purchases until you have a clear financial plan in place. High-interest debt can be financially draining. If you have existing debt, consider prioritizing payments on high-interest loans like credit cards.

10. Update Beneficiaries and Estate Planning

Update your beneficiaries on retirement accounts, life insurance, and any investment accounts to reflect your new marital status. Review your will, powers of attorney, and any trusts to ensure they align with your current goals and protect your family.

11. Keep Track of Your Credit Score

Divorce can impact your credit, so monitor your credit report to ensure it stays accurate. A strong credit score can help with future investments and loans if needed. If necessary, set up a plan to pay down any joint debt and, if possible, close joint accounts to protect your credit profile.

12. Automate Savings and Investments

Set up automatic transfers to your savings and investment accounts. Automating ensures consistency and keeps you on track with your financial goals. Start with small, regular contributions, and increase them over time as your financial situation stabilizes.

13. Reassess Your Financial Plan Periodically

As your life changes, so will your financial needs. Periodically review your budget, investments, and goals to ensure they're still aligned with your long-term plans. Keep educating yourself on personal finance and investment strategies so you can make informed decisions that support your financial well-being.

14. Consider Working with a Financial Planner

A certified financial planner (CFP) can provide tailored guidance based on your unique situation. They can help with long-term planning, especially if your divorce has significantly changed your financial picture.

Investing and saving during a divorce can feel daunting, but with a clear plan and gradual progress, you can set yourself up for financial security and growth in the years to come.

UNDERSTANDING RETIREMENT PLANS AND BENEFITS

Understanding retirement plans and benefits is a crucial part of long-term financial planning, especially during a divorce. Dividing retirement assets fairly and strategically can impact your financial future. Here's a guide to help you navigate the process effectively:

1. Identify All Retirement Accounts and Benefits

- **Make a List of All Retirement Assets:** Collect

information on all retirement accounts held by you and your spouse, including 401(k) plans, IRAs, pensions, and any other savings or investment plans related to retirement.
- **Look Beyond Obvious Accounts:** Don't overlook less common retirement benefits, such as profit-sharing plans, stock options, and deferred compensation plans. They may hold significant value and should be included in the asset division.

2. Determine the Value of Each Account

- **Request Statements and Documents:** Gather up-to-date statements for all accounts to understand their current balance and terms. Some accounts, like pensions, may require special documentation or actuarial calculations to estimate their present value.
- **Seek Professional Appraisal if Needed:** For pensions or complex investment accounts, consider hiring a financial professional to accurately determine their value. Understanding the worth of each asset will ensure a fair division.

3. Learn About Qualified Domestic Relations Orders (QDROs)

- **Understand QDROs for Dividing Qualified Plans:** A Qualified Domestic Relations Order (QDRO) is a legal order used to split certain retirement accounts, like 401(k)s and pensions, during a divorce. A QDRO allows funds to be divided without penalties.
- **Ensure Proper Filing:** Make sure the QDRO is filed correctly with both the court and the retirement plan administrator to ensure a smooth transfer of funds. An attorney or QDRO specialist can help you navigate this process.

4. Consider the Tax Implications

- **Be Aware of Taxable and Non-Taxable Accounts:** Different retirement accounts have varying tax consequences. For example, Roth IRAs grow tax-free, while traditional 401(k)s and IRAs are taxed upon withdrawal. Understanding these distinctions will help you make informed decisions about asset division.
- **Plan for Future Tax Liabilities:** Remember that funds you withdraw in retirement may be subject to income tax. Factor these taxes into your long-term financial planning and discuss options with a financial advisor.

5. Decide on Division or Trade-Offs

- **Evaluate Equal Splits vs. Trade-Offs:** Depending on your financial needs and future plans, you may choose to split retirement assets equally or agree to keep other assets (like the family home) in exchange for a lesser portion of retirement funds.
- **Consider the Long-Term Impact:** Dividing retirement assets can have a major impact on your financial future. Weigh the pros and cons of each option, and think about how each arrangement supports your retirement goals.

6. Update Beneficiary Information

- **Review and Update Beneficiaries:** After divorce, update beneficiaries on all retirement accounts to reflect your new wishes. This is essential to prevent your former spouse from inheriting assets unintentionally.
- **Consider Setting Up a Trust:** If you have children, you may want to set up a trust or designate a trusted family member as a beneficiary to manage these assets in the event of your passing.

7. Take Steps to Rebuild Your Retirement Fund

- **Open Your Own Retirement Accounts:** If you don't already have an individual retirement account, consider setting one up. Contributing to your own 401(k) or IRA will help you build financial security.
- **Maximize Contributions Over Time:** Depending on your income, consider maximizing contributions to tax-advantaged retirement accounts each year. This long-term habit can significantly improve your financial outlook.

8. Consult with a Financial Advisor

- **Get Professional Guidance:** Working with a certified financial planner or retirement specialist is highly beneficial. They can help you navigate the technical aspects of dividing retirement assets, develop a tax-efficient strategy, and identify new opportunities to grow your retirement fund.
- **Plan for Future Financial Goals:** A financial advisor can also help you reassess your post-divorce financial goals and adjust your retirement plans based on your current income, expenses, and lifestyle.

9. Factor in Social Security Benefits

- **Learn About Spousal Benefits:** If you were married for at least 10 years, you may be eligible to receive Social Security benefits based on your ex-spouse's record once you reach retirement age. This does not affect your ex-spouse's benefits and can be a valuable supplement to your income.
- **Plan Strategically for Social Security Timing:** Depending on your financial needs, you may choose to claim Social Security benefits early or delay them for a higher monthly payout. A financial advisor can guide you on the best timing based on your situation.

10. Reassess Your Retirement Timeline and Goals

- **Adjust Your Retirement Goals:** Post-divorce finances may change your timeline or retirement goals. Consider adjusting your retirement age, lifestyle, and savings targets to align with your current situation.
- **Focus on Rebuilding Financial Stability:** Prioritize financial stability and flexibility in your retirement plans. Reevaluate your income streams and explore additional savings strategies if needed.

By proactively planning and understanding your

retirement benefits and options during the divorce, you can create a stable foundation for your financial future. Careful preparation will help you move forward with confidence, knowing you're on track to reach your long-term goals.

CREATING A FINANCIAL SAFETY NET

Creating a financial safety net during a divorce is crucial to ensure stability now and long-term financial security as you move forward. Here's how to get started:

1. Build an Emergency Fund

Aim for 3-6 months of essential living expenses, which can cover housing, utilities, food, and transportation. Start with a goal of one month of expenses, then gradually build up. Keep this fund in a separate, easily accessible savings account, like a high-yield savings account, so you won't be tempted to dip into it for everyday expenses.

2. Evaluate Your Monthly Expenses and Create a Realistic Budget

Review your current expenses and income to understand your cash flow, including any child or spousal support you might receive or pay. Set up a detailed budget that prioritizes essentials first (housing, food, insurance, transportation) and limits discretionary spending. This will help you see where you can save or reallocate money to build your safety net faster.

3. Eliminate High-Interest Debt

If you have high-interest debt, such as credit card balances, work to pay it down as quickly as possible. High-interest debt can drain your finances and make it harder to build a safety net. Consider strategies like the snowball or avalanche method to reduce debt efficiently. As you pay off debt, you'll free up more money to allocate toward savings.

4. Set Up Separate Financial Accounts

If you previously shared accounts with your spouse, consider setting up new individual checking, savings, and investment accounts. This ensures clear control over your finances and keeps your assets separate. Having your own accounts helps prevent complications and miscommunications, making it easier to save and invest toward your personal goals.

5. Maximize Your Employer Benefits

If employed, review your benefits package. Contributing to a 401(k) or similar retirement plan can offer tax benefits and build long-term savings. Take advantage of other benefits, like health savings accounts (HSAs), dependent care accounts, or discounted life and disability insurance, to protect yourself and your family.

6. Prioritize Health and Disability Insurance

Health issues or injuries can be a significant financial setback. Make sure you have adequate health insurance coverage, especially if your marital status change impacts your coverage. If you're the primary income earner or support dependents, consider disability insurance. This provides income protection if you can't work due to illness or injury, adding an extra layer of security.

7. Automate Your Savings

Set up automatic transfers from your checking account to your savings and retirement accounts. This builds consistency and helps you prioritize saving without thinking about it. Start with small amounts if necessary and gradually increase as your financial situation stabilizes. Even a small contribution each month can grow over time, thanks to compounding interest.

8. Start a Retirement Fund or Continue Contributions

Ensure you're contributing to retirement accounts like a 401(k), IRA, or Roth IRA, even during the divorce process. Retirement savings will play a significant role in your future financial stability. If you need to divide retirement accounts as part of the divorce, consult with a financial advisor or attorney to understand the impact and possible tax implications.

9. Consider Life Insurance as a Safety Net for Dependents

If you have children or other dependents, consider taking out a term life insurance policy that would provide for them financially if anything were to happen to you. Life insurance can cover various needs, such as income replacement, education expenses, or other long-term support for your dependents.

10. Invest in a Diversified Portfolio for Long-Term Growth

Start a diversified investment portfolio, even if you're only able to contribute a small amount initially.

Investing over time can help grow your assets to meet future needs. Focus on low-cost, diversified options, like index funds or ETFs, which provide exposure to a wide range of assets and generally have lower fees than actively managed funds.

11. Stay Educated on Personal Finance

Educating yourself on personal finance, budgeting, and investing can empower you to make informed decisions. Books, podcasts, and online courses can help you understand concepts like risk tolerance, retirement planning, and tax strategies.

12. Regularly Review and Adjust Your Financial Plan

As your financial situation changes, revisit your budget, savings goals, and investment plan. Life changes, such as a new job or significant expenses, may require adjustments to your financial safety net. Try to review your progress every six months to ensure you're on track with your goals.

By taking these steps, you'll create a strong foundation that supports both immediate needs and long-term goals, helping you rebuild financial security and independence post-divorce.

Chapter 12: Embracing New Beginnings

CELEBRATING YOUR JOURNEY AND GROWTH

Celebrating your journey and growth during a divorce is a meaningful way to honor how far you've come, acknowledge the progress you're making, and build excitement for the future. Even amidst challenges, taking time to reflect on and celebrate yourself can help you embrace this new chapter with confidence and optimism. Here are some ways to approach this:

1. Acknowledge How Far You've Come

- **Reflect on Personal Growth:** Take time to look back on your journey and recognize the emotional strength and resilience you've

developed. Journaling about your experiences can help you see just how much you've grown.
- **List Your Accomplishments:** Write down the positive changes you've made—small and large. Whether it's setting boundaries, finding new independence, or rekindling interests, these are milestones worth celebrating.

2. Create Rituals for Letting Go

- **Have a 'Release' Ceremony:** Symbolically let go of your past by writing down things you're leaving behind (old hurts, insecurities, or limiting beliefs) and releasing them, perhaps by burning the list or tearing it up.
- **Redecorate Your Space:** Refreshing your home with new decor or simply rearranging furniture can create a symbolic "new beginning" in your surroundings. It allows you to make your space feel like an expression of the new you.

3. Celebrate with Loved Ones

- **Host a 'New Beginnings' Gathering:** If you feel ready, consider a small celebration with friends or family to mark this new chapter. Surrounding yourself with people who uplift you can remind you of your support network and fill you with positivity.

- **Share Your Journey:** Lean on friends or join support groups to share how you're evolving. Voicing your experiences helps solidify your progress and connects you with others who are on similar paths.

4. Set New Goals and Aspirations

- **Create a Vision Board:** Use a vision board to visualize your new dreams and goals. Include images and words that inspire you and represent the life you want to create for yourself moving forward.
- **Make a Personal Mission Statement:** Outline what matters most to you now—your values, goals, and aspirations. This statement will help keep you focused and motivated as you step into your new future.

5. Engage in Meaningful Self-Care

- **Treat Yourself:** Invest in self-care practices that feel like a reward—whether it's a spa day, a weekend getaway, or a new hobby you've wanted to try. Choose activities that replenish you and make you feel valued.

- **Celebrate Small Wins:** Take pride in your day-to-day victories, whether it's making a tough decision, sticking to a budget, or doing something outside of your comfort zone. Recognize these achievements as steps toward building a stronger version of yourself.

6. Explore Your Independence

- **Take Yourself on Solo Adventures:** Doing things alone can help you reconnect with yourself and build confidence. Try activities that feel empowering, like solo travel, going to a concert, or even taking yourself out to dinner.
- **Rediscover Old Hobbies or Try New Ones:** Reconnecting with hobbies or exploring new interests can bring joy and self-discovery. This is an opportunity to uncover new passions that enrich your life.

7. Embrace New Routines and Rituals

- **Establish a "New Beginnings" Ritual:** Create routines that remind you daily of your fresh start. Morning affirmations, evening gratitude reflections, or weekly planning sessions can help you feel grounded and motivated.
- **Set Weekly or Monthly Intentions:** Choose a

word or phrase that captures what you want to focus on each week or month (like "growth," "joy," or "self-love"). These intentions will guide you in your journey and serve as reminders of your progress.

8. Surround Yourself with Positivity

- **Curate a Positive Environment:** Fill your space with things that inspire you—motivational quotes, photos, or items that remind you of your progress. A supportive environment uplifts your spirit and reinforces your growth.
- **Connect with Like-Minded People:** Find support groups, friends, or mentors who inspire and encourage you. These relationships provide support and help you stay motivated as you embrace your new chapter.

9. Celebrate Progress Over Perfection

- **Forgive Setbacks and Keep Moving Forward:** Understand that healing isn't linear and that setbacks are a natural part of growth. Celebrate your resilience by accepting these moments and refocusing on your goals.
- **Focus on Your Journey, Not Just the Destination:** Remind yourself that personal growth is a

continuous process. Take pride in each step you're taking rather than just the end result.

10. Mark Your New Chapter with a Special Celebration

- **Do Something Symbolic:** Mark the transition with a symbolic gesture, like planting a tree, taking a solo trip, or writing a letter to your future self. This can represent both your strength and the beginning of a fulfilling new life.
- **Give Yourself a "New Chapter" Gift:** Whether it's something small or significant, treat yourself to a gift that symbolizes your fresh start. This could be anything from a piece of jewelry to a keepsake that reminds you of your journey.

By celebrating your growth and courage, you empower yourself to embrace this new beginning. These steps help you see the divorce as a transformative journey rather than just an ending, creating a foundation for the fulfilling and joyful life that awaits you.

SETTING LONG-TERM PERSONAL AND PROFESSIONAL GOALS

Setting long-term personal and professional goals during a divorce can be incredibly empowering, giving you direction and motivation as you move forward. Here's how to approach goal-setting in a way that embraces this new beginning and supports both your healing and future success:

1. Start with Self-Reflection

Take time to reflect on what's most important to you now, given your current circumstances. Consider what you value most in your life and what you want to prioritize. Identify areas of growth and ask yourself which aspects of your life—such as career, personal growth, relationships, or health—feel ready for development. This reflection will help you set meaningful goals aligned with the person you're becoming.

2. Set Realistic, Achievable Goals

Use the SMART goal framework to make sure your goals are Specific, Measurable, Achievable, Relevant, and Time-bound. Clear, practical goals keep you focused and give you a sense of control, which can be grounding during a challenging time. Start with Short-Term goals as stepping stones as goals can create momentum. For example, if your long-term goal is to improve your financial situation, a short-term goal could be setting a monthly budget. These smaller goals provide structure and confidence as you build toward bigger ambitions.

3. Create Separate Personal and Professional Goals

Define personal goals and think about areas like health, hobbies, relationships, or personal fulfillment. Examples might include taking up a new hobby, improving physical fitness, or rebuilding your social network. Consider the direction you'd like your career to take—whether it's seeking a promotion, learning new skills, or even changing industries. Think about ways your career could align with your fresh start and future plans.

4. Focus on Goals That Support Your Independence

Establish goals related to building financial stability, like creating a savings plan, paying off debt, or investing for the future. Financial goals can help you feel more empowered and secure. Consider goals that support your emotional well-being, such as creating self-care routines, building healthy boundaries, or learning new coping strategies. Emotional independence helps you become more self-reliant and resilient.

5. Break Goals Down into Manageable Steps

Create a step-by-step action plan for each goal, and outline smaller steps or milestones. Breaking down goals makes them feel more achievable and provides you with measurable progress to celebrate along the way. Give each step a timeline, which helps prevent procrastination and keeps you moving forward. Knowing when you plan to accomplish each part of your goal will help you stay organized and focused.

6. Visualize Your Future

Spend time imagining what you want your life to look like in 5–10 years. Envision your future self achieving these goals and living a life that feels fulfilling and joyful.

Create a Vision Board and collect images, quotes, or objects that represent your goals and the life you want to build. A vision board serves as a daily reminder of your aspirations and helps you stay inspired.

7. Prioritize Personal Growth and Self-Discovery

Explore goals like building self-confidence, improving communication skills, or increasing self-awareness. Personal growth goals enhance your ability to navigate future relationships and challenges. This is a time to learn and grow. Consider taking courses, reading books, or finding mentors who support your journey. Learning something new can open doors to opportunities you may not have considered before.

8. Create Goals Around New Beginnings

Embrace this fresh start by setting goals around exploring new places, trying new activities, or meeting new people. This can help you redefine your identity outside of marriage and discover passions you may not have pursued before.

Reaching out and building new relationships—whether a friendship, mentorship, or professional networking—can enhance your personal and professional life in positive ways.

9. Review and Adjust Your Goals Regularly

Reflect on your progress by setting a regular time, perhaps monthly or quarterly, to review your goals and assess your progress. This allows you to adjust as needed based on new experiences or changing circumstances. Allow yourself flexibility as life is unpredictable, and your needs may shift as you continue through your divorce. Don't hesitate to revise goals that no longer resonate with you, and permit yourself to set new ones as your priorities evolve.

10. Celebrate Small Wins Along the Way

Recognize and celebrate your accomplishments, no matter how small they may seem. Rewarding yourself for each step helps you stay motivated and reinforces that you're making meaningful progress.

Treat yourself with kindness and patience. Goal-setting is a journey. Be gentle with yourself, especially if things take longer than expected. Remember, you're building a fulfilling future one step at a time.

11. Visualize Your New Identity and Embrace the Process

See yourself as the person who's already achieved these goals. How does this future version of you feel, think, and act? Visualizing yourself as already successful strengthens your confidence and belief in your abilities.

Enjoy the journey of rediscovery as setting and

working toward new goals can feel liberating. Embrace the process as an opportunity to explore, grow, and thrive in ways that are uniquely meaningful to you.

Embracing long-term goals while navigating a divorce gives you purpose and direction. By focusing on what you want to achieve personally and professionally, you're building a foundation that supports not just recovery, but a fulfilling and empowered future. This is your chance to dream big, create a life that reflects who you are, and celebrate the resilience you've gained along the way.

FOSTERING A POSITIVE OUTLOOK ON LIFE

Embracing new beginnings during a divorce can be challenging, but fostering a positive outlook can make all the difference in finding peace and joy again. Here are some ways to help you cultivate that positivity:

1. Focus on Self-Care and Well-being

Prioritize your physical, mental, and emotional health. Activities like exercise, meditation, journaling, or simply taking quiet moments for yourself can help you process emotions constructively. Treat yourself with kindness and patience. Adjusting to change takes time, so allow yourself to feel and heal without judgment.

2. Surround Yourself with Positive Support

Lean on friends, family, or a support group that offers encouragement and understands your journey. Sharing with people who genuinely listen can provide comfort and validation. Avoid those who focus on negativity, and try to build a network of people who uplift you and inspire hope for the future.

3. Set Personal Goals for Growth

Think about who you want to become and set goals that excite and motivate you, whether it's learning a new skill, advancing in your career, or simply taking up a hobby you've always wanted to try. Focusing on personal growth can help you shift from dwelling on the past to building a future that reflects your authentic self.

4. Practice Gratitude Daily

Make it a habit to write down three things you're grateful for each day, even small things like a sunny morning or a good cup of coffee. Gratitude shifts your mindset from what's lacking to what's present in your life, helping to cultivate a positive outlook.

5. Embrace Your New Independence

View this period as an opportunity to rediscover yourself and build a life that aligns with your passions and dreams. Embracing independence can feel empowering and liberating. Reframe challenges as chances to learn and grow, which helps reinforce a sense of resilience and confidence in handling life's changes.

6. Allow Yourself to Let Go of Resentment

Forgiveness—whether for yourself or your ex-partner—can be freeing. Letting go of resentment allows you to move forward without carrying the weight of past hurts.

Focus on acceptance. Realize that letting go of past expectations opens space for new possibilities.

7. Envision a Bright Future

Picture yourself happy and fulfilled in the future. Visualization helps shift your focus toward what's possible and motivates you to work toward a life that excites you. Set small, achievable steps to make that vision a reality, building confidence and positivity along the way.

8. Practice Mindfulness and Stay Present

Mindfulness helps you focus on the present rather than dwelling on the past or worrying about the future. This can reduce stress and increase appreciation for everyday joys. Engaging fully in what's happening now—whether it's a conversation with a friend or a walk in nature—can bring you moments of peace and happiness.

9. Celebrate Your Strengths and Progress

Acknowledge each step you take, big or small, as progress. Recognize the resilience, courage, and growth you're building with each step forward. Celebrate even the smallest victories, which can reinforce a sense of self-worth and reinforce a positive mindset.

10. Find Purpose in New Beginnings

Use this transition as a time to reflect on what truly matters to you. Define your purpose, whether it's related to family, career, personal goals, or a passion you've set aside. Pursuing what gives your life meaning provides direction and helps you feel empowered to move forward.

By embracing these practices, you'll gradually cultivate a positive outlook that not only helps you navigate your divorce but also sets the stage for a fulfilling new chapter in life. Remember, every step you take toward positivity and self-care is a step toward a happier, more empowered future.

Epilogue

As you turn this final page, remember that you are stronger, wiser, and more resilient than you may realize. Divorce is not just an ending—it's a chance to rebuild, redefine, and embrace a new beginning. This journey may have felt daunting at times, but each step has brought you closer to a life that is truly yours, crafted by your courage and guided by your inner strength.

Throughout this book, you've explored your emotions, taken practical steps, and begun to reclaim your sense of self. You've faced difficult truths, navigated uncertain territory, and shown a determination that will continue to serve you. Remember, healing is not a linear process. Some days will feel easier than others, and that's okay. Allow yourself the grace to move at your own pace.

As you continue forward, keep in mind that you are not defined by your past but by the person you choose to become. Embrace this next chapter with an open heart and the knowledge that you are capable of creating a fulfilling, joyful, and empowering life. Surround yourself with people who uplift you, lean on the resources that support you, and always remember that you are worthy of happiness, peace, and love.

This journey may have started with uncertainty, but from here on out, it's a story of hope, renewal, and boundless possibility. I am honored to have been a part of your journey, and I hope this book serves as a source of guidance and strength as you move forward. You are never alone on this path—your resilience and spirit will light the way.

About The Author

Lijwana Washington

Lijwana is a dedicated self-publisher, writer, and advocate for women's empowerment. With a background that combines practical life experience and a deep passion for helping others, Lijwana brings a unique and heartfelt perspective to her work. Having navigated the challenges of divorce firsthand, she  understands the emotional and practical hurdles women face during this transformative period. Lijwana's own journey through divorce was a profound experience that inspired her to create the kind of guide she wished she'd had—a comprehensive resource to support, uplift, and empower women as they rebuild their lives. Driven by her desire to make a difference, she poured her insights and knowledge into this book, offering a compassionate voice and practical tools to help women move forward with strength and clarity. When she's not writing, Lijwana enjoys designing, organizing gatherings that foster connection and community, and traveling—a passion that fuels her own spirit and reminds her of the beauty and possibilities that lie beyond life's challenges. Through her work, Lijwana hopes to be a source of inspiration and guidance, helping women recognize their resilience and embrace their new beginnings with confidence.

www.ingramcontent.com/pod-product-compliance
Lightning Source LLC
Chambersburg PA
CBHW070148100426
42743CB00013B/2847